Eastbourne
CONCOURS d'ELEGANCE

A celebration of automotive design on the Sussex coast

1930-1937 motor shows

Stephen LeVine

Cover photo from the Eastbourne Local History Society archive.

First published 2026
Published by Loncastle South
Eastbourne, U.K.
e-mail: loncastlesouth@yahoo.co.uk
website: www.stephenlevine.co.uk

British Library Cataloguing in Publication Data. A catalogue record of this book is available from the British Library.

ISBN: 978-0-9935441-8-7

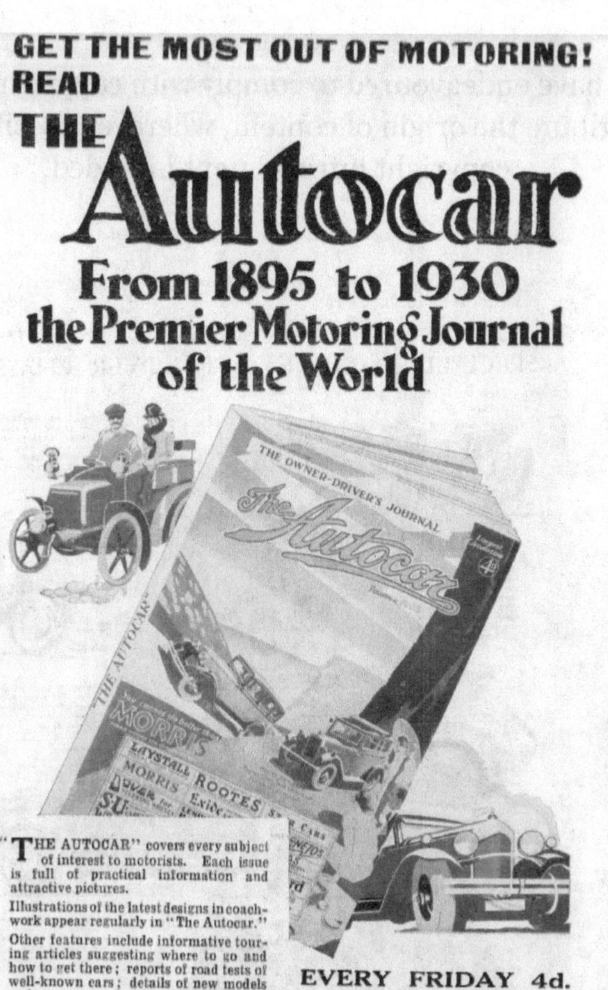

The Autocar advert 1930

DISCLAIMER

I have endeavoured to comply with copyright and to attribute the origin of content, wherever possible. No copyright infringement intended.

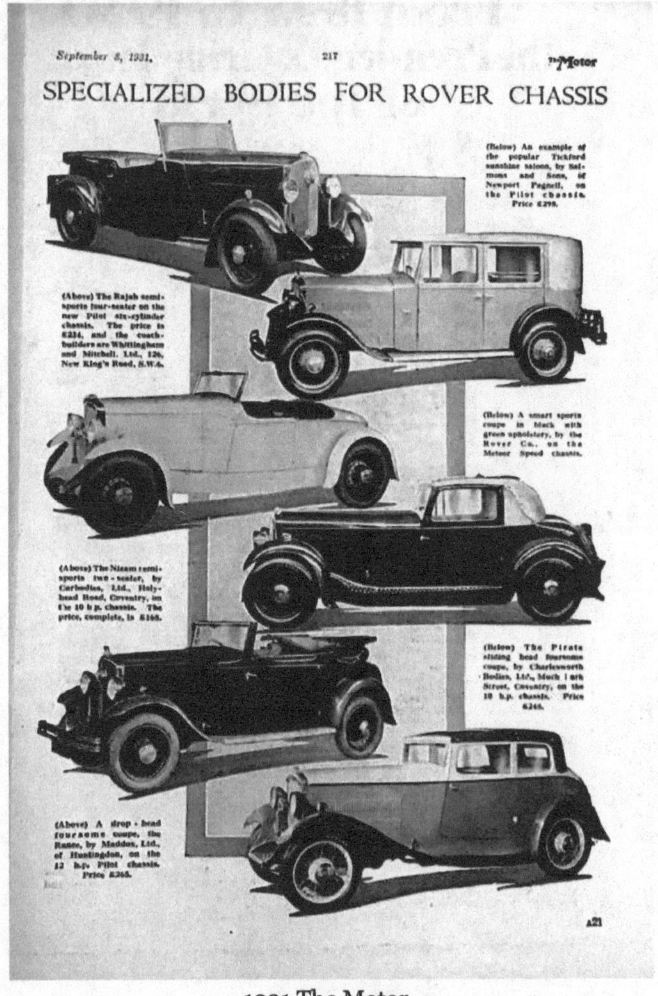

September 8, 1931. 217 The Motor

SPECIALIZED BODIES FOR ROVER CHASSIS

(Below) An example of the popular Tickford sunshine saloon, by Salmons and Sons, of Newport Pagnell, on the Pilot chassis. Price £298.

(Above) The Rajah semi-sports four-seater on the new Pilot six-cylinder chassis. The price is £234, and the coachbuilders are Whittingham and Mitchell, Ltd., 126, New King's Road, S.W.6.

(Below) A smart sports coupe in black with green upholstery, by the Rover Co., on the Meteor Speed chassis.

(Above) The Nizam semi-sports two-seater, by Carbodies, Ltd., Holyhead Road, Coventry, on the 10 h.p. chassis. The price, complete, is £168.

(Below) The Pirate sliding head foursome coupe, by Charlesworth Bodies, Ltd., Much Park Street, Coventry, on the 10 h.p. chassis. Price £245.

(Above) A drop-head foursome coupe, the Rance, by Maddox, Ltd., of Huntingdon, on the 12 h.p. Pilot chassis. Price £265.

A21

1931 The Motor

The Motor magazine sponsored the first Concours events in England.

Table of Contents

September 1921, Dinard, Brittany, France.

The first recognised Concours d'Elegance

D. Cabart

Madame Watney driving her Delage at Dinard

ACKNOWLEDGMENTS

Thank you to everyone who provided information and photographs for this publication. Special thanks to Eastbourne Library, East Sussex Records Office (ESRO), The National Archives, the online newspaper archives, Eastbourne Local History Society (E.L.H.S.), the National Motor Museum (N.M.M.), and Simon Williams for editorial guidance.

1. INTRODUCTION

Concours d'Elegance (the French term that translates as a competition of elegance) is a motor show that celebrates the history and beauty of motor vehicles. These events focus on judging classic and vintage cars for their craftsmanship, appearance, and overall presentation. By bringing together enthusiasts and specialists, they helped build a community and a sense of pride in the latest car designs. Among the British towns that held shows, Eastbourne's events were among the earliest and longest-running pre-war competitions, and the town gained a national reputation for innovation and elegance. Eastbourne's unique contribution to shaping the Concours tradition in Britain makes its story particularly significant in both local and national history, and it is an interesting story in its own right.

This introduction outlines the origins of the Concours d'Elegance motor shows, examines their development in Britain in the early 1900s, and explores the growth of Eastbourne's events before the war.

In the 1930s, the Concours d'Elegance events played an increasingly significant role in British motoring history. As cars became more affordable and technology advanced, these competitions provided a platform for the latest ideas in engineering and design. Both professionals and skilled individuals took part, reflecting the British love of innovation, comfort, and quality. Well-known manufacturers, coachbuilders, and members of fashionable society attended, showing the era's interest in progress and elegance.

These events also shaped public taste, encouraged new features, and improved the image of motoring. A clearer understanding of these events can be gained by first examining their historical development.

Concours d'Elegance events date back to the 17th century in France, when aristocrats in the summer exhibited their latest ornate horse-drawn carriages by hosting parades and viewings for fellow members of high society in the Paris parks and gardens.

As cars became more common, this tradition of showing off originality and elegance moved from horse-drawn carriages to motor vehicles. This legacy still lives on in today's car shows.

Focusing now on the motorcar era, reports from the Fédération Française des Véhicules d'Époque (FFVE) state that the town of Dinard, in Brittany, France, hosted the world's first recognised and recorded motorcar Concours d'Élégance on 4 September 1921. The event featured vintage and historic cars. André Beck de Fouquières, a well-known columnist and author, conceived the idea and assembled a respected panel of judges. This panel included HRH the Grand Duke Kirill Vladimirovich of Russia, Count Emmanuel de la Rochefoucauld, Marquis de Montferrer, Madame Blériot, and other prominent Europeans. Beck de Fouquières served as the committee's chairman and established the first competition rules. For more details on the event, refer to the FFVE archives report number 1921-01-Dinard.

One hundred vehicles joined the rally, and 30 cars competed. Pierre Durand-Ruel, son of the well-known art dealer and Impressionist patron Paul Durand-Ruel, won the event in a beautifully presented Voisin fitted with a Gaston Gillotte body.

In the early events, they weren't just competitions but occasions for the elite to show off their newly custom-built vehicles. Surprisingly, women drove most of the cars on display, even though the owners were men.

The judging criteria, which focused on the car's craftsmanship, design, authenticity, and appearance, may explain this.

The judges also considered the elegance of the women presenting the vehicle and the complete harmony of the presentation.

Over the years, these shows have brought together car manufacturers, coachbuilders, and fashion designers. They have attracted spectators from the industry, fashion, and the arts, with the public eager to examine the machines on display.

This first show was a great success, attracting many tourists to the town. Soon, similar events started across Europe, in Monte Carlo, Rome, and beyond.

In Britain, towns like Bexhill, Brighton, and Lewes were also early leaders in motorsport.

Bexhill calls itself the 'Birthplace of British Motor Racing' because it hosted the Automobile Club of Great Britain's time trials on Galley Hill by the sea on 19 May 1902. The race was open to British and international entrants. The French driver Leon Serpollet, in his Gardner-Serpollet steam car, "Easter Egg," won the race, which is widely regarded as Britain's first motoring competition.

Following Bexhill's example, in July 1905, Brighton staged Speed Trials along the seafront on Madeira Drive.

Almost two decades later, in September 1922, Eastbourne held speed trials along the seafront, sponsored by the Eastbourne Motor Club. Around the same time, in Lewes, the Brighton and Hove Motor Club hosted motorcycle and car speed trials on Race Hill, with its first meeting held on July 27, 1924.

The Society of Motor Manufacturers and Traders (S.M.M.T.) was formed in 1902 and, the following year, held the first British Motor Show at London's Crystal Palace from 14 to 22 February.

There was growing public interest in motor cars alongside recent advances in the UK motor industry. Many car enthusiasts travelled abroad to attend and take part in car events.

In the 1920s, organisers of motor events in Britain routinely linked Concours d'Elegance events with rallies, races, or local gatherings to judge the coachwork and elegance of the latest motor cars. As a result, these events grew in popularity and soon became a regular part of the British motoring calendar.

According to The Motor Magazine, the first open-to-all Concours d'Elegance in the UK was held in July 1928. The Hampshire Automobile Club, with Lord Montague of Beaulieu as president, organised the event in collaboration with the magazine. In 1952, the Montagu family founded the National Motor Museum at Beaulieu, Hampshire.

Organisers held this first event over three days in Bournemouth. Mr A.E. Morgan, a local garage owner and club member, suggested the idea at a Town Council meeting in April 1928.

Motor clubs and fundraising organisations often organised similar gatherings in the 1920s. For example, the Bexhill Cottage Hospital Fund hosted a Monster Fun Fair with a small Concours d'Elegance for motor cars on 14 August 1929. The competition featured three classes: one for cars costing less than £200, another for cars between £200 and £500, and the last for vehicles costing £500 or more. There were four judges: two men and two women. Mr H.J. Mulliner, a well-respected coach builder, was one of them. This show was a minor event, with mainly residents participating. In 1930, they organised a similar event.

Bexhill's first recognised motor car Concours d'Elegance competition took place in July 1934.

On 30 June 1939, Brighton hosted a Concours d'Elegance on Madeira Drive as part of its Brighton Gala Week.

<u>Bournemouth: Britain's First Public Concours, 1928.</u>

Bournemouth was, in fact, the first town in England to host a Motor Rally and Concours d'Elegance on public roads, open to the public as competitors and spectators. They had support from The Motor Magazine, the Royal Automobile Club, and the S.M.M.T.

The event took place on Thursday, Friday, and Saturday, July 5, 6, and 7, 1928. It was a three-day affair followed by a grand dinner at Bournemouth's town hall, hosted by the mayor.

Motorcycles, combinations, and three-wheelers were not allowed. On Saturday, they held the judging of the Concours d'Elegance on East Overcliff Drive.

There were 18 vehicle classes, 12 classes for specific makes, plus special classes for women drivers, with many attending from high social backgrounds. This was truly an international show with competitors coming from Britain, America, and the Continent. More than 268 entries took part in the competition. Some British entries came from as far away as John o' Groats and rural Wales and Cornwall.

The show featured vehicles ranging from a Morris Minor and an Austin 7 to a Lagonda and a Rolls-Royce. Miss Lorenzo from London won Class 1, open cars under £250, with her 1922 11.9 h.p. Morris-Cowley. A 6-cylinder, 32-34 h.p. drop-head coupé Minerva with Martin Walker coachwork won first prize in the £800 to £1,500 car category.

Mrs Victor (Mildred Mary) Bruce, a well-known British record-breaking racing driver, powerboat racer and pilot, won first prize in Class 15 and the Ladies Cup in her blue AC Acedes motor car.

In the evening, they had a dance, and during the intermission, they presented the prizes. Dancing ran from 8 to 11:45 p.m., with tickets costing 4s. 6d., which included refreshments.

The show was a great success for the town, bringing in many visitors who stayed in the town's hotels.

In August 1928, the Illustrated Sporting and Dramatic News reported that Southend planned to organise a Motor Rally and a Concours d'Elegance.

However, the S.M.M.T. refused to approve the event due to limited local support, unlike the enthusiasm shown at the Bournemouth show.

Shortly after Bournemouth's event, the second show to be held in England was the Southport International Motor Rally and Concours d'Elegance, which took place from 20 to 23 September 1928, with competitors starting from John o'Groats, Land's End, Paris, Brussels, and other towns.

Organised jointly by the Southport Motor Club and The Motor magazine, and supported by the Automobile Association, which was responsible for marshalling and parking, the show attracted support from across the continent. It received more than 250 entries across eight classes. Entrants could choose one class for each vehicle they entered. The Concours show on Saturday, 22nd, was open to private competitors and traders and supported by the Society of Motor Manufacturers & Traders. Judging took place on Saturday morning, and the winning cars paraded along the promenade on Sunday afternoon. One of the oldest cars on display was a twenty-year-old Rolls-Royce owned by Mr T. Haley of Harrogate.

Thirty-three judges, among whom were Viscount Curzon and Sir Walter Windham, inspected the vehicles and awarded the show prizes. The winner of the silver cup, presented by the Southport Corporation for the best car in the Concours event, was a Lanchester straight-eight. It also won the best-in-class award. Another winner in her white Ballot was Miss Paddy Naismith, an actress, pilot, and racing driver who was reported to be Britain's first air hostess.

The Lanchester Straight Eight

THE winner of the 150-guinea Silver Trophy for the finest Car entered in the Great International Motor Rally and Concours d'Elégance, held at Southport in September, and also of the Premier Prize for the best Car in its class. It offers a new experience in safe, high-speed, luxurious motoring.

Particulars as to delivery dates, bodywork, etc., on request. Trial runs by appointment.

Armourer Mills, Birmingham. | 95, New Bond Street, London, W. | 88, Deansgate, Manchester.

Spectators could park their cars along the sands off the promenade for 6d per car.

In January 1929, newspapers reported that the S.M.M.T. had banned traders from attending Motor Rallies and Concours d'Elegance events. The S.M.M.T. argued that the expense incurred was the reason for this decision. It also stated that it disagreed with the view that members should support these events. In reply, the R.A.C. stated that it issues permits for events, whether open to the public or closed club events, and that the S.M.M.T. has no jurisdiction. Without S.M.M.T. support, organisers would face financial difficulties and would need to make other arrangements.

The S.M.M.T. subsequently lifted the ban after forward-thinking manufacturers and dealers informed them that they saw significant commercial value in attending these events and in advertising winning entries.

<u>The origins of the Eastbourne Concours</u>

Having set this historical background, we now examine the history and progression of Eastbourne's Concours d'Elegance from 1930 to 1938, the pre-war period. We show how the Eastbourne event brought together a varied automotive community, set standards of elegance, and helped shape the reputation of British motor shows. In these shows, the emphasis was on new and current cars, unlike today's shows.

It was not until 1929 that Mr Miles Thompson, who had recently returned from France after attending a motor show there, proposed to Councillor C.H. Taylor of the Residential Hotels and Caterers' Association the idea of organising a motor car Concours d'Elegance event in Eastbourne.

This group, which organised the Eastbourne Carnival and Beauty Pageant, saw an opportunity to attract more visitors to the town and adopted the idea. In 1930, Eastbourne hosted its first show, enlisting the help of prominent members of the motoring community.

In September 1930, shortly after adopting the idea, Eastbourne held its first show under the S.M.M.T. and R.A.C. regulations. Soon after, other towns, including Hastings, Bexhill, Torquay, Bristol, Blackpool, Cardiff, and Ramsgate, held their own shows.

Eastbourne became one of the first towns to host this type of competition, with backing from the local council and support from traders under the Motor Traders' Regulations. The show quickly established itself as the leading motoring event of the 1930s.

The organisers sent entry forms to all competitors, along with a list of regulations for the upcoming show. Eastbourne's competition welcomed all car owners, whether they drove an expensive Rolls-Royce, a modest Austin, or a Morris.

After judging, they awarded a red rosette to the winners and a blue rosette to those finishing second. They presented prizes and trophies later in the day. The organisers also awarded special prizes for local residents and lady drivers.

Soon, Eastbourne gained a reputation as the first show to display the latest models unveiled by motor manufacturers.

Captain Eric Short, the organising secretary, said that the virtue of this kind of show is the opportunity for motorists of all types to meet other enthusiasts, share ideas and experiences, observe cars they have not seen before, and exchange ideas in the world of motoring. Capt. Short played a major role in the success of the Eastbourne shows.

These early shows were considerably different from today's events. They retained the original idea of featuring the latest vehicles from various coachbuilders, with their owners proudly displaying any additional accessories fitted to the models.

Motor manufacturers regularly supplied only a chassis to a client, who would then instruct a coachbuilder to build a body to the owner's taste. This could be for a Rolls-Royce or a sports car.

As one motoring magazine said, "The show should be truly elegant in every sense of the word. Cars should be judged for the sheer beauty of their lines and colour scheme, and on the perfection of their finish. Those exhibiting them should be as well-dressed and as smartly turned out as their cars."

1928 Southport

SEPTEMBER 28, 1928. 509 THE LIGHT CAR AND CYCLECAR

SOUTHPORT'S CONCOURS D'ELÉGANCE

Austin Swallow entered by Henly's Ltd and won best in class.

Photographer unknown.

Mrs Victor (Mildred Mary) Bruce, winner in Class 15, in her blue AC Acedes motor car.

2. 10 SEPTEMBER 1930

In 1928, Mr Miles Thompson, owner of Eastbourne's Park Gates Hotel, first proposed that Eastbourne host a Concours d'Elegance for motor cars. He had recently returned from the south of France, where he attended the Élégance et Automobile à Monte-Carlo show, which was a great success. Thompson believed a similar event in Eastbourne would considerably boost the town's reputation and popularity, so he contacted Councillor C.H. Taylor of the Angles private hotel, a fellow member of the Residential Hotels and Caterers' Association, who was interested in learning more about the idea. After lengthy discussions, it took 18 months to decide to proceed with the plan. A committee was then set up to organise the event, with Councillor C.H. Taylor as chairman and Captain Eric I. Short of Mansfields Motor Company as deputy, alongside 12 other members.

Captain Short, who served with the Royal Army Service Corps (RASC) during World War I, was forced to leave the army due to an injury. He moved to Eastbourne in 1922 and worked for various motor businesses and would be the mainstay of Eastbourne's motor shows over the next seven years.

Eastbourne hosted the third recognised Concours d'Elegance in Britain and the first to be sponsored by the local council and tradespeople. Organisers hoped the new event would attract more visitors and enhance the town's reputation.

Initially, the plan was to include the Concours d'Elegance as part of Eastbourne's August carnival.

However, after receiving feedback, the committee decided to hold it as a separate event.

They agreed to hold it on Wednesday, 10 September, during Motor Week, which raised funds for Princess Alice Memorial Hospital.

The event was open to privately owned and trade vehicles from Eastbourne and other towns. Trade vehicles were a new feature.

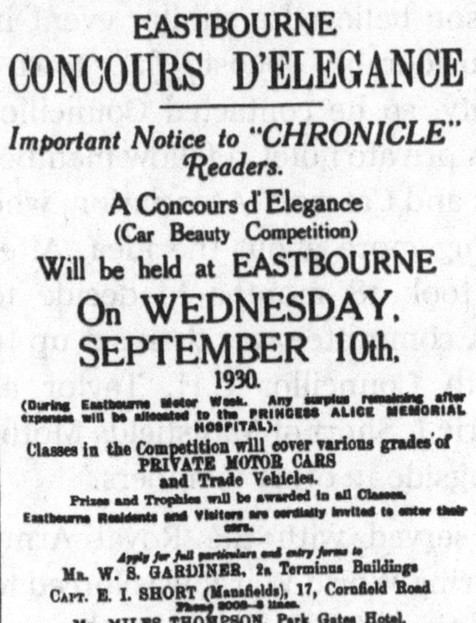

EASTBOURNE
CONCOURS D'ELEGANCE

Important Notice to "CHRONICLE" Readers.

A Concours d'Elegance
(Car Beauty Competition)
Will be held at EASTBOURNE
On WEDNESDAY,
SEPTEMBER 10th.
1930.

(During Eastbourne Motor Week. Any surplus remaining after expenses will be allocated to the PRINCESS ALICE MEMORIAL HOSPITAL).

Classes in the Competition will cover various grades of
PRIVATE MOTOR CARS
and Trade Vehicles.

Prizes and Trophies will be awarded in all Classes.
Eastbourne Residents and Visitors are cordially invited to enter their cars.

Apply for full particulars and entry forms to
MR. W. S. GARDINER, 2a Terminus Buildings
CAPT. E. I. SHORT (Mansfields), 17, Cornfield Road
Phone 2008—3 lines.
MR. MILES THOMPSON, Park Gates Hotel.

Entries Close September 3rd, 1930.

Eastbourne, already a premier holiday destination, hoped the new event would attract more British and international visitors to the town.

The committee secretary, Captain Eric Short of the motor retailer Mansfields, Cornfield Road, Eastbourne, pledged to donate surplus funds to Princess Alice Hospital. During Motor Week, volunteer collectors would travel around town collecting funds for the hospital.

The organisers wanted Amy Johnson, the famous pilot, to attend the show, but she was unable to do so because of prior commitments. She had already visited Eastbourne in August, when Mr P. Rossi presented her with a Beachy Head Lighthouse car mascot.

Patrons of the first show were Eastbourne's Mayor, Lt-Col. R.V. Gwynne, D.S.O., D.I., J.P.; Rt. Hon. Earl Howe, C.B.E., V.D., and Edward Marjoribanks, the town's M.P.

There were special classes for trade, special, and private cars. Some criteria for classifying the vehicles on display were whether they were open or closed cars.

Organisers also divided the vehicles into categories based on cost: under £200, £201-£1,200, and over £1,200. The classes of motor cars ranged from Class A to Class J. Competitors could enter multiple classes, and the organisers encouraged them to do so.

The classes for the show are:

A. Open cars costing £200 and under.

B. Closed cars costing £200 and under.

C. Open cars costing from £200 to £500

D. Closed cars from £200 to £500.

E. Open cars from £500 to £800.

F. Closed cars from £500 to £800.

G. Open cars from £800 to £1,200.

H. Closed cars from £800 to £1,200.

J. Closed cars from£1,200 and over. Park Gates Hotel Challenge Bowl.

L. Smartest and best-kept delivery van.

M. Smartest and best-kept lorry.

N. Smartest and best-kept open char-a-banc.

O. Smartest and best-kept closed char-a-banc.

There were also classes for the smartest car of any value owned by an Eastbourne resident (P1) and for a bona fide Sussex resident (P2). The most distinctive vehicle of any value was in class Q. Class R was for the smartest and best-kept car, with age taken into account. All entrants would receive a class card and number to attach to the front of their vehicle.

Awards included cash prizes, banners, mascots, trophies, and a prize for the car driven by the prettiest woman.

Entry fees were 5 shillings for the trade section and 10 shillings and 6 pence for other classes.

Among the 20 judges was the well-respected Captain Malcolm Campbell, D.S.O., the land and water speed record holder and motoring correspondent.

Organisers hoped his presence would highlight the event's prestige and attract motor enthusiasts. Other well-known attendees included Capt. C.D. Barnard, a long-distance record pilot; Capt. N. Stack, A.F.C., a stunt pilot; Sir Alan Cobham, K.B.E., A.F.C., the pioneer airman; Lady Cobham; Mr R.V. Stanley of Bexhill; and Earl Howe, a racing driver and credited as one of the founders of the British Racing Drivers Club.

The judges would award points for the condition of the engine, chassis, equipment, and fittings, as well as the vehicle's age. They would also assign points for seating comfort, colour scheme, and general condition. During their inspections, three or four marshals, police, and A.A. personnel accompanied the judges to keep back crowds and allow the judges to examine the cars freely.

Under "General Appearance", the judges gave marks for the overall design, bodywork style, and the character of the finish. Under "Condition", the judges would consider the age and the function of the vehicles. This was most appropriate for the trade vehicles. The judges were to follow the "Cleanliness of engine and chassis" aspect strictly. The maximum score in each category was 25 points.

Messrs Bentleys Ltd, Messrs William Bruford & Sons Ltd, The Sussex Daily News and The Motor magazine had generously donated silver cups for the winning entrants.

The Ford Motor Co. Ltd. also donated a silver cup for the best-kept Ford passenger car and another for the best Ford commercial vehicle.

Organisers were thrilled with the response to their invitations, as it was fantastic, with 120 vehicles entered into the competition. They asked all entrants to arrive at Devonshire Place by 10:45 a.m., as judging was set to begin at 11:30 a.m. Mr B.F. Bovill, the chief marshal, assigned the vehicles their positions. He lined up the cars along both sides of the road, allowing judges to walk around each car and carry out thorough inspections. Lines of bunting and flags stretched from the trees in Devonshire Place, welcoming visitors.

Competitors came from all over Britain, including one who drove down from Berwick-upon-Tweed in Northumberland, England's northernmost point.

Initially, the public was to remain on the pavements, but due to the large number of visitors, the marshals lifted the restriction, allowing the public to move freely.

At this inaugural show, besides Sir Alan Cobham, the aviator, the judges included Earl Howe, C.B.E., V.D.; Colonel P.T. Etherton; Major R.V. Stanley; Captain R. Twelvetrees, A.M.I. Mech E. (judging the trade vehicles); Captain Michael Campbell, D.S.O.; and Captain Hartman (involved with Concours d'Elegance in England and on the Continent). Additional judges were Gertrude Lady Decies, a society writer for the Daily Mirror; Captain W. Lawford, a pilot; Mr Cecil Kimber, managing director of M.G. Cars; Captain C.D. Barnard, a renowned long-distance flyer; Mr S.C.H. Davis, a racing car driver and writer for the "Autocar"; Mr Robert Little; Mr H.E. Symons, a writer for the "Motor"; Mr L. Cushman, a racing car driver; Mr L. Clayton; Mr Percy Ellison, A.M.I.M.E., manager of the Eastbourne Corporation Motor Bus Department, assisting Captain Twelvetrees; and Mr E. Infield Willis.

Mr Miles Thompson hosted lunch at the Park Gates Hotel for the judges and chief officials.

After the judging, which concluded in the late afternoon, the judges awarded red and blue rosettes to all winning entrants. The committee then arranged for Councillor C.H. Taylor and Mr Miles Thompson to present a silk banner embroidered with the words 'Eastbourne Concours d'Elegance' to the winners in the private classes. Arrangements were made for Lady Cobham to present the trophies and prizes on the lawns near the Wish Tower between 4:15 p.m. and 4:45 p.m.

Capt. Short's young three-year-old son, Roland Eric, riding a toy aeroplane, presented a bouquet of freshly picked carnations to Lady Cobham.

After the presentations concluded, competitors paraded in column formation around the town and along the seafront. The parade ended on the Western Lawns opposite the Grand Hotel. A table had been set with the prizes, and Lady Cobham presented the awards to the winners.

The newspapers reported that more than 10,000 people lined the seafront to watch the cars pass by.

Following the prize-giving, the test pilot and aviation pioneer, Capt. T. Neville Stack, A.F.C., performed an aerobatic display, flying over the sea.

Captain Stack was recognised as a world-famous test and stunt pilot and was the first to fly from London to Delhi in a light aeroplane.

Thankfully, the weather at the show was perfect.

Capt. N Stack

There was only a light morning shower followed by clear skies and sunshine.

All the owners displayed their cars in top condition, with some having sent their vehicles to coach builders for extra cleaning.

The Clifton Hotel hosted a grand dinner for judges, chief marshals, and workers after the show.

Attendees gave speeches, thanked the organisers and judges for the successful event, and expressed a hope they could repeat the show next year.

Sir Alan Cobham, the aviation pioneer and one of the judges, proposed that the town could also host a Concours d'Elegance for aeroplanes. Eastbourne Council was considering building an aerodrome, but advisors told them it would cost about a quarter of a million pounds. The Council had not yet made a decision.

After the show, everyone agreed it had greatly benefited the motor trade and the town and recommended making the event an annual occurrence.

There were forty-four trade entries in this first show. Southern Glideway Coaches Ltd. of Seaside, Eastbourne, was proud of its achievements at the show, having won a first prize for best-kept open motor coaches, and second prize for best-kept closed motor coaches. They placed a large advertisement in the Eastbourne Gazette on 17 September. Meanwhile, Eastbourne Motors Ltd, the Ford dealership, announced in the Eastbourne Chronicle on 30 September that Ford vehicles had won silver cups.

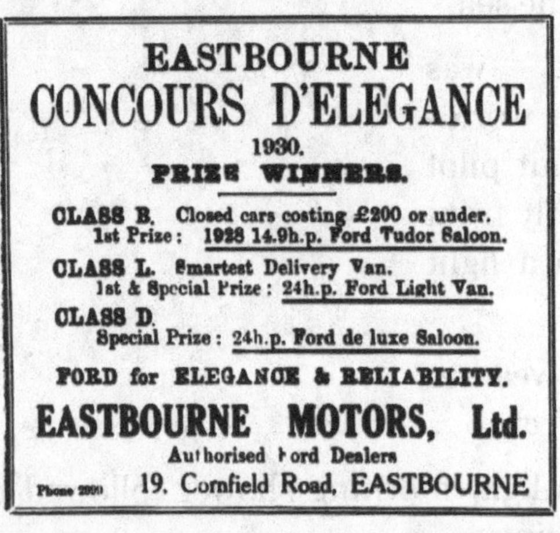

See Appendix I for a full list of the prize winners.

The Motor/LAT

Mrs J.A. Mackle in her 1930 Hoyal-bodied Daimler. Class G winner.

The Motor/LAT

Major Willoughby-Osborne, entrant 120, with his 1930 Farina-bodied Lancia Dilambda coupe. Winner in class H and P.2.

Eastbourne
Concours D'Elegance

Official Programme

September 10th, 1930

PRICE SIXPENCE

First prize: a 14 cm-high silver cup, hallmarked Birmingham, won by Lord De Clifford in his 1930 2-litre Lagonda.

The Motor

Mrs Churchill Wylie with her Rolls-Royce, winner of The Motor Cup.

3. 9 SEPTEMBER 1931

Compared to the inaugural Concours d'Elegance in 1930, Eastbourne's second annual event in 1931 showed marked growth and new ambitions. Not only did the number of classes and entries increase, but the organisers also introduced additional features, such as a special veteran car rally in partnership with the London 'Veteran Car Club.' In January, a committee met to confirm the second Concours d'Elegance in Eastbourne, following the success of the previous year's show. They appointed Capt. Eric Short as the organising secretary.

Patrons of the show this year were the mayor of Eastbourne, Lt-Col. R.V. Gwynne, D.S.O., D.L., J.P., the Rt. Hon. Earl March; the Rt. Hon. Earl Howe, C.B.E., V.D.; and Edward Marjoribanks, M.P.

This year's event took place on Wednesday, the 9th of September, and the competition invited entries in 23 classes. Entry fees for this year's show were 5s for veteran cars, 7s 6d for cars under £350, and a guinea (£1. 1s) for vehicles over £350.

The judges scored all entrants out of 100 marks. For private cars, the criteria were the elegance of the lines (25), seating comfort (25), colour scheme (15), and cleanliness of the engine and chassis (15 marks). For commercial vehicles, the criteria were general appearance (15), special features for service and utility (40), condition (30 marks, considering age and function), and cleanliness, engine, and chassis (15 marks).

Judges evaluated the veteran cars based on the vehicles' age, history, original condition, and the cleanliness of their engines and chassis.

Organisers have rearranged the classes for this year's show.

As before, there was a trade section with three classes and a 10s 6d entrance fee: their classes were X: delivery vans, the smartest and best kept; Y: lorries, the smartest and best kept; and Z: motor coaches (closed), the smartest and best kept.

The classes for motor cars attending the show are:

A. Closed cars costing up to £150.

B. Open cars costing up to £150.

C. Closed cars from £151 to £250

D. Open cars from £151 to £250.

E. Closed cars from £251 to £350.

F. Open cars from £251 to £350.

G. Open and closed cars from £351 to £450. H. Open and closed cars from £451 to £800.

I. Open and closed cars from £801 to £1,000.

J. Open and closed cars from£1,001 to £1,700.

K. Open and closed cars over £1,700. L. Open and closed sports cars under £500.

M. Open and closed sports cars over £500.

N. Smartest car of any value owned by an Eastbourne resident.

O. Smartest car of any value owned by a Sussex resident.

P. Most distinctive car of any value.

Q. Best kept owner-driven car when age and mileage will be taken into account.

R. Best kept chauffeur-driven car when age and mileage will be taken into account.

S. Veteran cars no later than 1904.

There were also four classes for cars that had won a first award in any Concours d'Elegance in Great Britain or on the Continent in 1930 or 1931.

T. Open and closed cars valued up to £500.

U. Open and closed cars valued from £501 to £1,000.

V. Open and closed cars over £1,000.

W. For the most distinctive open or closed car of any value.

In 1931, the organisers received over 285 forms from interested parties and 193 entries for the competition. The motoring magazines reported that the show was the country's largest this year.

Additionally, this year, the Veteran Car Club organised a special rally on Tuesday, 8th September, for pre-1904 vehicles. The starting point was Croydon Aerodrome, with cars departing at 9 a.m. at one-minute intervals.

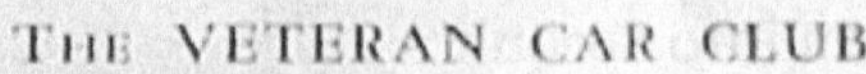

THE VETERAN CAR CLUB

PRESIDENT · S. C. H. DAVIS

London-Eastbourne Rally

Held under the General Competition Rules of the R.A.C.

IN CONNECTION WITH

EASTBOURNE CONCOURS D'ELEGANCE

SEPTEMBER 8th-9th, 1931

Starting at 9 a.m.

Official Programme

3[D.]

ENTRIES
DRIVERS
ROUTE MAP

Daily Mirror

Mr. E. O. Hobden's 20 h.p. Armstrong Siddeley, with body by Young and Co., which won first prize in Class 1.

The Motor

Cars travelled from London to Eastbourne via East Grinstead, Maresfield, Uckfield, Hailsham, and Polegate, covering 51½ miles. The finish line was at the top of Chalk Pit Hill, Willingdon.

After all competitors arrived, they drove down Upperton Road to Eastbourne Town Hall, where they met the mayor, Col. R. Gwynne, and Captain E.I. Short.

By June, 30 cars had signed up. The R.A.C. and A.A. agreed to help with marshals and organisation in London. At East Grinstead, 19 miles from the start, all drivers stopped for 45 minutes.

Organisers instructed everyone to park on Portland Road by the Dorset Arms Hotel. If needed, vehicle repairs could be carried out during the break.

Upon reaching Eastbourne, and after Lady Foley presented a commemorative plaque to the successful drivers, the competitors prepared their cars for entry into the Concours, which created a special class for them.

On Tuesday evening, between 4 and 6:30 p.m., the drivers parked the veteran cars in a designated enclosure at Gildredge Park, where the public could inspect the vehicles for a fee of 6d.

Nearly a thousand people turned out to admire the old veteran cars. That evening, all the cars were taken to the Whitley Road Garage for secure overnight storage.

Mr I. Martin, in a 30-year-old 60-hp four-cylinder Mercedes, was the first to reach Eastbourne in record time: one and a half hours, averaging 34.32 miles per hour. Mr R.S.C. Beresford's 1901 12 h.p. Fiat came second, and Mr A.H.R. Forlden's 1903 18 h.p. Mercedes third.

An 1894 Benz 12 h.p., driven by Mr G. James Allday, was the oldest car to finish, and he came in 16th out of 27 finishers.

The organisers instructed all cars and trade vehicles to assemble in Devonshire Place by 11 a.m., with judging scheduled to start at 11:30 a.m. Due to the large number of cars this year, the judging did not finish until 4:30 p.m.

Judges for this year's show were Captain Sir Malcolm Campbell, D.S.O.; The Rt. Hon. Earl Howe, C.B.E., V.D.; Mr C.L. Clayton, A.R.I.B.A.; The Rt. Hon. Earl of March; Sir Alan Cobham, K.B.E., A.F.C.

Also, Lieutenant-Commander Montague Grahame White, Major C.M. Picethorn, M.C., Flight-Lieutenant C. Clarkson, Mr F.T. Bidlake, Flight-Lieutenant H.M. Schofield, Mr Leon Cushman, Captain W. Lawford, Captain R. Twelvetrees, Mr S.F. Edge, Mr H.E. Symons, Captain J.S. Critchley, Mr J.W. Stocks, Lieutenant-Colonel W.C. Bersey, a pioneer of electric vehicles and a founding member of the R.A.C., Mr H.J. Mulliner, Mr J.R. Chaplin, and Mr C. Douglas Clease, B.Sc., a writer for The Autocar.

Mr Miles Thompson hosted a lunch for the judges and officials at the Park Gates Hotel.

The weather had been brilliant, with sunshine all day, and after the judging, the cars paraded through the town.

To everyone's delight, the veteran vehicles led the motor parade along Cornfield Road, Terminus Road, Seaside Road, and Cavendish Place to the pier, then along Carlton Road and back along the Parade. Viscountess Lady Ratendone presented seven cups and other prizes to the class winners on the Western Lawns opposite the Grand Hotel.

TO-DAY

(Wed., Sept. 9th)

Concours d'Elegance

IN

DEVONSHIRE PLACE,

EASTBOURNE,

followed by a

SPECIAL DANCE

at the

GRAND HOTEL,

9.15 p.m. to 12.30 a.m.

TICKETS obtainable at Entrance to Ballroom 7/6

As last year, there was an air display over the seafront, performed by Flight Lieutenant Christopher Clarkson, Aviation Manager at Selfridge & Co. Ltd., and Flight Lieutenant H.M. Schofield, test pilot for General Aircraft Ltd at Croydon aerodrome. Thousands of spectators gathered along the promenade to watch the aerobatic display.

Donors of Prizes

The Lady Foley	Silver Salver
Miss Elizabeth Bolton	Silver Cup
Miss Elizabeth Bolton	Silver Plaque
"The Autocar" ...	Voucher, value £5 5s. 0d.
Veteran Car Club	Silver Cup
Trinidad Leaseholds, Ltd.	Silver Cup
"The Motor"	Silver Cup
"Sussex Daily News"	Silver Cup
"Mentor," the Tobacconists ...	Silver Cup
J. H. Bartlett, Esq.	Silver Cup
Vigzol Oil Co., Ltd.	Prize
Lubricien Oil Co., Ltd.	Prize
"Eastbourne Gazette" and "Herald" ...	Prize
"Eastbourne Chronicle"	Prize
R.O.P., Ltd.	Prize
F. J. Parsons, Ltd.	Prize
H. Parkinson, Esq.	Prize
Smith & Tugwell	Prize
Formans, Compton Street	Prize
A. F. Bobby & Co., Ltd., ...	Prize
Cavendish Hotel	Prize
Grand Hotel	Prize
A. E. Wilcox, Esq....	Prize
Bell Insurance Co.	Prize
The Mostyn Hotel...	Prize
Universal Insurance Co.	Prize
Boots the Chemists	Prize
Veteran Car Club	Prize
Parkinson, Polson & Co., Ltd.	Prize
Mr. & Mrs. Geoffrey Stubley	Prize

Page Two

N.M.M.

Toasts

HIS MAJESTY THE KING

To Propose - - Mr. Miles Thompson

THE JUDGES

THE COMMITTEE OUR HOST

To Propose - His Worship the Mayor of Eastbourne

(Lt.-Col. R. V. Gwynne, D.S.O., D.L., J.P.)

THE JUDGES

To Respond - The Rt. Hon. the Earl of March

The Rt. Hon. the Earl Howe, P.C., C.B.E., R.D., V.D.

Sir Alan Cobham, K.B.E., A.F.C.

Sir Malcolm Campbell, D.S.O.

THE COMMITTEE

To Respond - - Mr. C. H. Taylor

Captain E. I. Short

OUR HOST

To Respond - - - Mr. Miles Thompson

Menu

Melon de Paris Rafraîchi

Paupiettes de Sole Park Gates Hôtel

Perdreaux Rotis

Pommes Gaufrettes Salade

Charlotte Russe

Fromage

Café

le 9 Septembre, 1931

N.M.M.

The Autocar

Class winner

F/Lt. Clarkson flew a twin-engine Gipsy De Havilland Moth, while F/Lt. Schofield flew a 75-h.p. Comper Swift Pobjoy. Both aircraft had been adapted for aerobatics.

After another successful show, the organisers held a grand dinner at the Grand Hotel, with the mayor presiding. Sir Alan Cobham, Lieutenant-Commander White (a founding member of the R.A.C.), and the mayor of Croydon, Alderman T. Arthur Lewis, all gave speeches congratulating Eastbourne on such a fine event. In Lt-Cdr White's speech, he said, "This is the finest and best organised Concours d'Elegance I have ever attended." After dinner, the guests danced inside the hotel ballroom to the Westenders Band.

The judges awarded competitors marks for any useful or unusual additions to their cars, and one of the show's most astonishing accessories must surely be a toilet outfit built into the luggage carrier.

They installed this essential addition on Mrs Church-Wylie's Rolls-Royce.

Mrs Church-Wylie's other entry, a 1923 Armstrong Siddeley, won second prize in Class Q and was reported to still be running on its original six spark plugs after 94,538 miles.

Class W winner. Mrs Gough's MG The Motor/LAT

1931 MG F type Magna.

The September issue of The Motor magazine stated that this year's show “was far and away the most successful event of this kind ever held in the British Isles.” They also said the cars on display were better turned out, better finished, and more luxurious and expensive than at any similar event in the country.

Lady Foley won the prize for the smartest car of any value owned by a bona fide Eastbourne resident, in her black and red Rolls-Royce.

Skinners of Western Road, Hastings, specialists in quality cars, supplied Mr J. Carter with his 20/25 h.p. Rolls-Royce. The car won first prize in Class O, which recognised the most distinctive vehicle of any value owned by a bona fide Sussex resident at the Eastbourne show.

Skinners were proud of their achievement and placed a large advertisement in the Hastings and St. Leonards Observer on 19 September.

THIS BEAUTIFUL 20/25 h.p. ROLLS ROYCE, property of Mr. J. Carter, secured FIRST PRIZE in Class "O" at the CONCOURS D'ELEGANCE held at EASTBOURNE on Wednesday, September 9th, 1931.

Class "O":—"For the most distinctive car of any value owned by a bona fide Sussex resident."

•

The above car was supplied by

SKINNERS

. 18, Western Road .

ST. LEONARDS-ON-SEA

'Phone HASTINGS 628

Who Specialize in Quality Cars

See Appendix II for a complete list of the prize winners.

Lady Foley Prize Giving　　　　　　　　Light Car & Cyclecar

H. L. Wardle in his M.G. four seater.

Autocar/LAT

Harold Heal's 1931 Rolls-Royce on parade.

Light Car & Cycle/LAT

Mr H.H. Anspach's Austin 7 Swallow receiving his award.

4. 7 SEPTEMBER 1932

The third show in Eastbourne took place on Wednesday, 7 September, at Devonshire Place, with over 140 entrants. This year, there were fewer large, expensive cars, but plenty of light cars were on display. The event included classes for both moderately priced and luxury cars, giving each a fair chance to win. There was a large trade contingent, with major motor manufacturers represented, including Rootes, Ford, Delage, Bedford and Chevrolet.

Organisers arranged the vehicles along both sides of Devonshire Place, leaving space for thousands of spectators to walk around and view the cars. All competitors had to be in position by 10:15 a.m.

This year's show had the approval of the Motor Manufacturers and Traders, and there was a display of new vehicles for visitors to browse. 1932 was an important year for the motor trade, with innovations in engines and gears that made it particularly significant for both the motor industry and car enthusiasts.

Some recent winners of the International Alpine Trial, known as one of the toughest tests for cars, were also on public display, but we're not taking part in the competition. Present was Donald Healey, who drove his 3-litre Invicta Tourer and became famous for his endurance and strategic navigation on difficult roads, earning legendary status in motorsport. Also on display was Lt.-Com. C.R. Whitcroft, R.N., who, with expert precision and daring skill, had recently won the R.A.C. International Tourist Trophy Race in his Riley Six.

Alongside them, the Armstrong Siddeley, driven by C.D. Siddeley, demonstrated remarkable reliability and performance in its class.

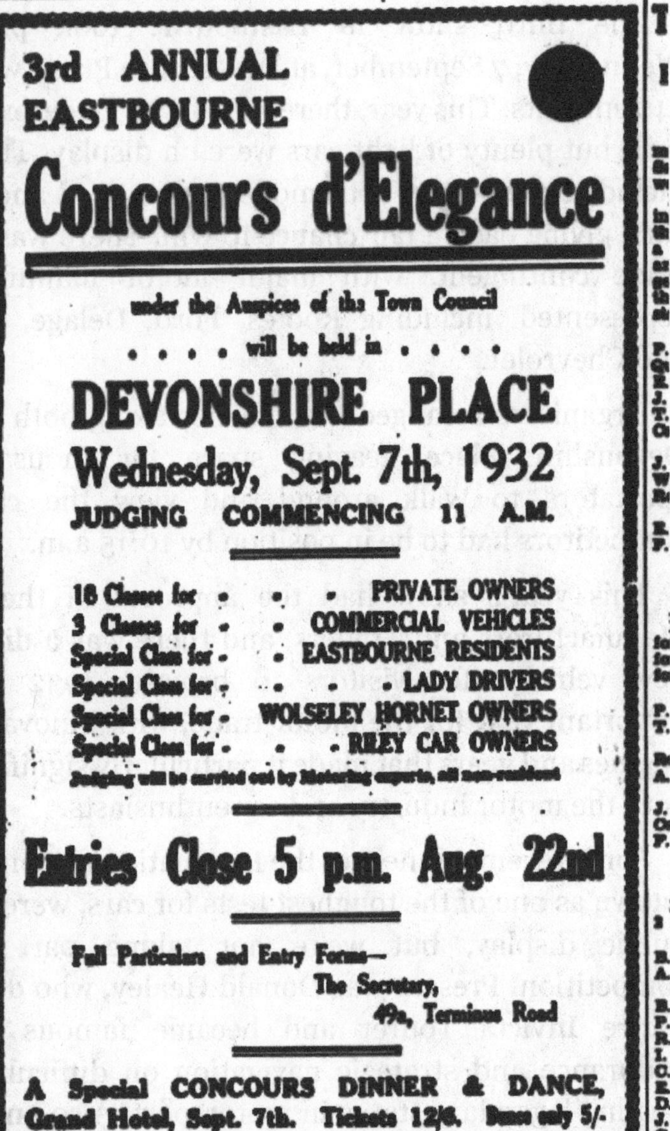

There were 18 classes for private cars, 14 for trade, and three for commercial vehicles. There were also four special classes for Eastbourne residents, lady drivers, Wolseley Hornet owners, and Riley owners.

Captain Sir Malcolm Campbell also entered his Blue 25 h.p. 1932 Rolls-Royce with Gurney-Nutting bodywork in one of these classes.

Maximum marks for this year's contest in general classes were: elegance of appearance (30), comfort (25), internal condition (10), external condition (15), cleanliness of the engine (5), internal convenience (5), and accessibility of the tool-kit and battery (10 marks). For commercial vehicles, the judges awarded marks for general appearance (20), general condition (30), service and utility features (40), and engine cleanliness (10 marks).

Classes 1 to 18 were reserved for privately owned cars, while classes 19 to 32 were open to motor manufacturers, coach builders, and motor agents. Classes 33 to 35 were for commercial vehicles and closed motor coaches. This year, some attendees expressed concern that private classes included trade entries. Others criticised the organisers for excluding lower-priced cars costing under £150, such as the Morris Minor and the Austin Seven, from the competition. These controversies sparked heated debates between participants and organisers. Some argued that trade entries in private classes gave professional competitors an unfair advantage, overshadowing individual enthusiasts.

Meanwhile, the exclusion of lower-priced vehicles drew criticism for failing to reflect the motoring community's diversity.

This triggered debates about whether the event maintained its traditional values of showcasing a wide range of vehicles and if it might discourage participation from enthusiasts with modest means. Due to these intense discussions and concerns, the organisers revisited the rules for the following year. With general approval in 1933, they expanded the eligible classes and reintroduced lower-priced cars into the competition, aiming to restore inclusion and encourage greater participation.

The organisers struggled to balance these different viewpoints, aiming to keep the event inclusive while maintaining its prestigious reputation.

Instructions to competitors were clear: "All vehicles had to assemble in Devonshire Place by 10:15 a.m., with their class card and numbers attached to the front of their cars. Judging would commence at 11 a.m. After the awards were presented, all participants would tour around the town."

The patrons of the show included the mayor of Eastbourne, Councillor Lachlan MacLachlan, J.P., Lt.-Col. R.V. Gwynne, D.S.O., D.L., J.P.; Captain Sir Malcolm Campbell, D.S.O., K.B.E.; The Rt. Hon. Earl Howe, C.B.E., V.D.; John Slater, M.P.; and W. Stranger-Jones.

The classes for motor cars attending the show are:

1. Closed cars cost from £150 to £250.
2. Open cars costing from £150 to £250.
3. Closed cars costing from £251 to £350.
4. Open cars costing from £251 to £350.
5. Open and closed cars costing from £351 to £500.

6. Open and closed cars costing from £501 to £700.

7. Open and closed cars costing from £701 to £1,000.

8. Open and closed cars costing from£1,001 to £1,500.

9. Open and closed cars costing over £1,500. Park Gates Hotel Challenge Bowl.

10. Open and closed sports cars costing up to £350.

11. Open and closed sports cars over £350.

12. Smartest car of any value owned by an Eastbourne resident.

13. Smartest car of any value owned by a Sussex resident.

14. Most distinctive car of any value.

15. The smartest car owned and driven by a lady.

16. Best kept car driven and maintained by a chauffeur.

17. The smartest and best-kept Riley car, owner-driven and maintained.

18. The smartest and best-kept Wolseley Hornet car, owner-driven and maintained.

19. Closed trade cars costing from £150 to £250.

20. Open trade cars costing from £150 to £250.

21. Closed trade cars costing from £251 to £350.

22. Open trade cars costing from £251 to £350.

23. Open & closed trade cars costing from £351 to £500.

24. Open & closed trade cars costing from £501 to £700.

25. Open & closed trade cars costing from £701 to £1,000.

26. Open & closed trade cars costing from £1,001 to £1,500.

27. Open & closed trade cars costing over £1,500.

28. Open and closed sports cars costing up to £350.

29. Open & closed sports cars costing over £350.

30. The most distinctive trade car up to £500 in value.

31. The most distinctive trade car over £500 in value.

32. The most distinctive trade car with specialised coachwork.

33. Smartest and best-kept delivery vans.

34. Smartest and best kept lorries.

35. Smartest and best kept closed motor coaches.

This year's judging panel included a diverse group of experts, each with a unique set of expertise. The Rt. Hon. Earl of March and the Hon. Brian Lewis judged classes 10 and 11. Col. Lindsey Lloyd, C.M.G., M.B.E., judged classes 7 to 9, and Lt-Com. Montague Grahame White, R.N., oversaw classes 12-14. Racing driver Capt. Sir Henry Birkin, along with Capt. F.W. Hartman gave their judgment on classes 7, 8, and 9.

The panel also included pilots, automotive editors, and engineers, such as Flt-Lt. C. Clarkson, who judged classes 5 and 6, and H.C. Lafone, editor of The Autocar magazine, who judged classes 19, 22, and 23. Mr R.F. Bovill was again the chief marshal.

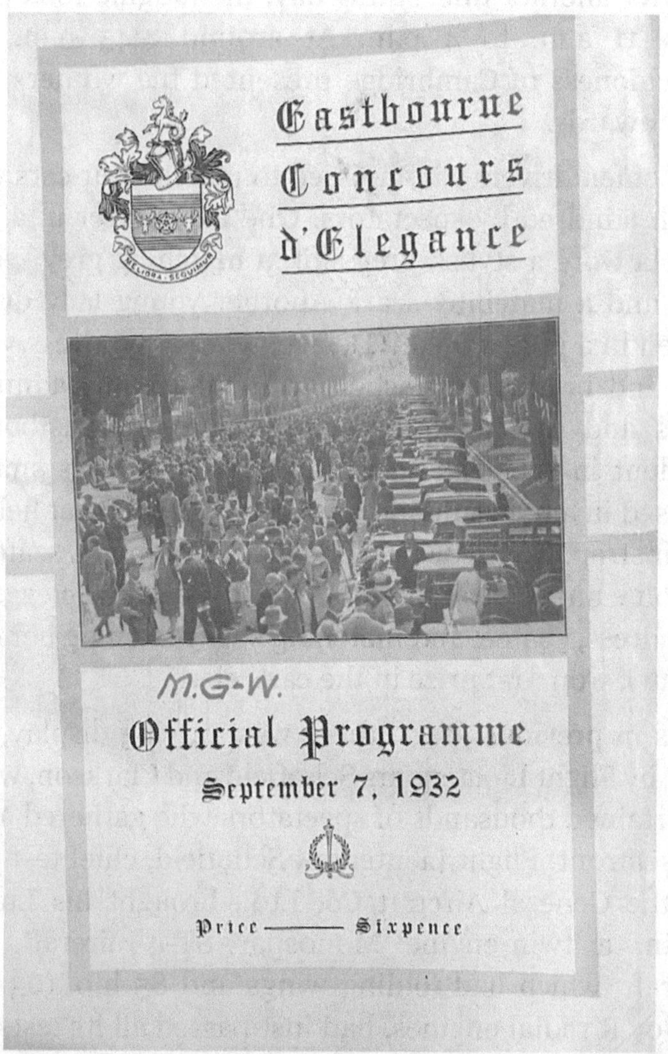
Eastbourne Concours d'Elegance

M.G-W.

Official Programme

September 7, 1932

Price —— Sixpence

N.M.M.

This year, The Motor magazine's trophy was a 31 cm Art Déco silver-plated statue of a dancing lady, mounted on a marble base. Once again, the Cavendish Hotel hosted a lunch for the judges and show officials.

After another fine, sunny day, the judging took place from 11 a.m. to 4 p.m. At around 4:45 p.m., the Marchioness of Cambridge presented the winners with their awards.

Women drivers who dressed to match their cars were much admired by spectators. One lady driver in a grey Lancia wore a stylish grey suit, a matching grey sequin cap, and a matching scarf. Another young lady driver, seated in a grey-and-red Delage, wore a red dress, a red hat, and bright red lipstick, attracting many admiring looks and causing quite a sensation. An Eastbourne resident in a black-and-white touring car was smartly dressed in a blue suit and a white felt pillbox hat held by a chinstrap. Not to be outdone, Lady Campbell, seated in her blue and silver Rolls-Royce and wearing an eggshell blue dress, coatee, and matching cap (matching her car's colour), won first prize in the car's class.

As in previous years, there was a flying display, this time by Flight Lieutenants Schofield and Clarkson, which entertained thousands of spectators who gathered along the seafront. Flight Lieutenant Schofield, chief test pilot for the General Aircraft Co. Ltd., brought his Luxury Cabin, a twin-engine Monospar ST-4 aircraft. The aircraft, which had folding wings and 85 h.p. (63 kW) Pobjoy R radial engines, had just passed all its tests and was being shown outside of London for the first time.

COUNTY BOROUGH of EASTBOURNE

EASTBOURNE

CONCOURS d'ELEGANCE

OFFICIAL
DINNER
AND
DANCE

SEPTEMBER 7th, 1932

CHAIRMAN:
HIS WORSHIP THE MAYOR of EASTBOURNE
(Mr. Councillor L. MACLACHLAN, J.P.)

N.M.M.

The event ended with a dance and dinner at The Grand Hotel. Tickets cost 12/6d for both or 5/- for just the dance, which started at 9 p.m.

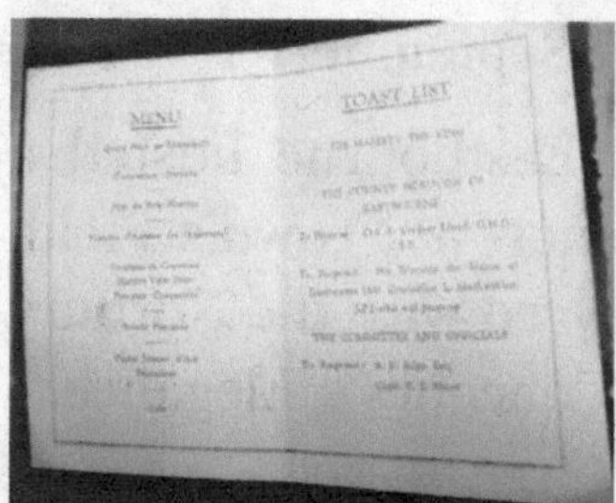
MENU

TOAST LIST

Third Annual
Eastbourne Concours d'Elegance

Dinner & Dance
at
The Grand Hotel, Eastbourne
On Wednesday, September 7th, 1932
7.30 for 7.45

Ticket, 12/6 Evening Dress

Some cars on display had interesting features, such as a 20 h.p. Royal blue with black top Armstrong Siddeley entered by Warwick Wright Ltd., (entrant 108) fully equipped for sport. In the rear box were four sets of polished-wood golf clubs, a pair of tennis racquets, tennis balls, and guns. Inside, the car revealed a different kind of elegance—a fold-out card table, ready for a game, with freshly dealt cards laid out. These details made the Armstrong Siddeley a symbol of refined leisure and sporting activity.

Another Armstrong Siddeley had silver bodywork, and silver-coloured leather also covered the interior. They called her the "Silver Sphinx." After the show, the London Armstrong Siddeley agents displayed the car in their Bond Street showroom.

One saloon car had a small water tank and a washbasin installed. Another had a combined tea canteen and cocktail bar in the boot.

Graham's, a car dealer in Amersham, placed an advert in the 23 September edition of the Bucks Examiner.

The advert announced that Armstrong Siddeley cars had won three first prizes and one second prize at the Eastbourne show. Sir Malcolm Campbell owned one of the cars that won first prize.

A motor dealer in Tunbridge Wells placed a similar advertisement in The Courier on 9 September.

On the August bank holiday, Eastbourne hosted a grand motor gymkhana and air show at Frowd's Field, King's Drive. Capt. Short was involved with the Norbury Motor Club in organising a small Concours d'Elegance.

Later in the year, the December issue of the Sussex Express carried an advertisement from The Bexhill Motor Co Ltd for a 1933 Standard saloon, "Little Twelve", for sale at £165.

The car belonged to Mr A.H. Oxenford and had recently won first prize in the £150 to £250 class at the Eastbourne show.

See Appendix III for a full list of the prize winners.

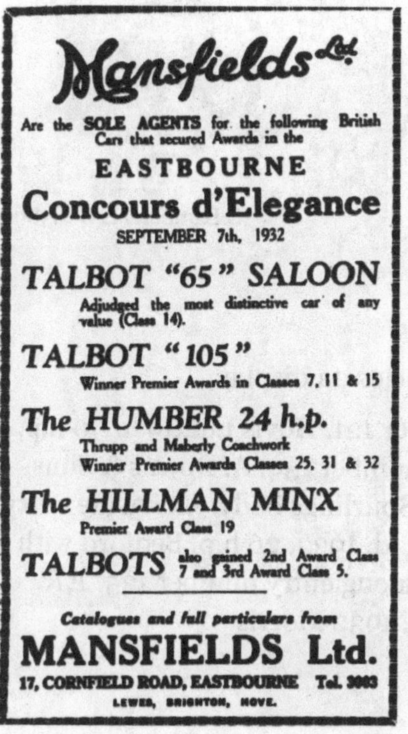

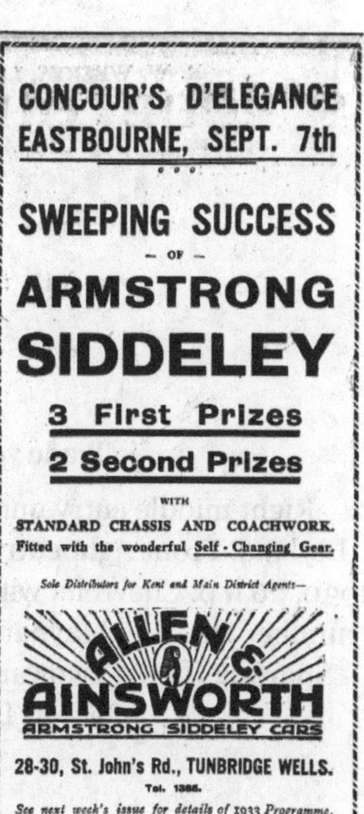

C.Lambert/LAT E3896

Trade vehicles on display.

Right middle entry number 121. Hovis Ltd. 1929 90 h.p. Leyland. Front right entry number 134. A. Downs & Sons, 1930, 26 h.p. Chevrolet with Spurlings body. Alongside entry number 116. G.E. Maynard Ltd, 1932, 26 h.p. Bedford with Spurlings body. Two vans along entry number 125. T.R. Beckett Ltd, 1932 Morris.

A 31cm tall Art déco silver-plated trophy featuring a dancing lady on a marble base with a plaque.
The trophy, inscribed "Eastbourne Concours D'Elegance 1932," was presented by The Motor magazine and awarded to Mr J.E. Scott for victory in his Talbot 65.

THIS LADY AT THE CONCOURS D'ÉLÉGANCE, EASTBOURNE.
FOR CARRYING A COCKTAIL-BAR IN HER CAR.

The Sketch Sept. 1932

The Marchioness of Cambridge presenting his trophy to A. H. Oxenford, whose 1933 12 h.p. Standard saloon with Standard coachwork, won the prize in the class for closed cars costing between £150 and £250.

Light Car & Cyclecar

Light Car & Cyclecar

ELEGANT SPORTS MODELS. — A group of competitors lined up for the Open Car class costing from £151 to £250. The winning car was the farther of the two Wolseley Hornet Swallows.

"ELEGANCE" AT EASTBOURNE. —— *The parade of cars following the Concours d'Elegance at Eastbourne (fully reported in this issue). The leader is a Wolseley Hornet which won the class for open cars costing between £251 and £350.*

1932 Light Car & Cyclecar

Shown by the manufacturers—the M.G. Midget with body by Carbodies, which came second in the £350 open and closed class.

Light Car & Cyclecar/Lat

5. 14 JUNE 1933

1933 was an important year for Eastbourne, marking the 50th anniversary of its Charter of Incorporation. The town officially became a municipal borough on 1 June 1883. To mark the occasion, the council organised events from Monday, 12 June to Sunday, 18 June. These included a Carnival and the Battle of Flowers (both on Thursday, 15 June), the Concours d'Elegance for motor cars (Wednesday, 14 June), an Air Rally and display (Friday, 16 June), and a Grand Military Tattoo (Saturday, 17 June). 1933 also marked the fourth consecutive year that Eastbourne hosted the motor show. This year, the Municipal Committee arranged all events.

Captain E.I. Short organised this year's motor event, ably assisted by Mr Edgerton as secretary and Mr B.F. Bovill as Chief Marshal. Mr H. Parkinson and Chief Inspector Harris of the A.A. acted as assistant marshals.

In earlier years, Eastbourne Council often discussed whether to build an airfield and to organise a Concours d'Elegance for aeroplanes. These debates reflected the national trends of the early 1930s. Advances in aviation and popular air events prompted many British towns to consider constructing municipal airports to promote growth and modernisation. Other towns in south-eastern England shared similar ambitions. This demonstrated a regional effort to lead in aviation during a period of rapid change and rising public interest in motoring and flight. Expressing his support and explaining his reasons, Captain Short wrote a two-column article, which the Eastbourne Chronicle published on Saturday, April 29.

To mark the Jubilee year, organisers moved the motor show from its usual September date to June to coincide with the anniversary celebrations.

The council advertised the events nationwide in advance, seeking to attract more competitors to the June schedule.

This year, Sir Malcolm Campbell, the internationally renowned racing driver who held multiple world land speed records, brought his record-breaking 2,600 h.p. 'Bluebird' to Eastbourne, where it was on public display. He also served as a steward at the event. Reid A. Railton, a leading automotive engineer who designed the 'Bluebird,' accepted an invitation to serve as one of the judges.

Additionally, on loan from the M.G. Car Co. Ltd. and displayed at the exhibition were M.G. Magnette K3 racing cars belonging to Capt. George Eyston and Earl Howe—both prominent figures in British motorsport. Notably, these cars had recently finished first and second in the light car class and also won the team prize in the challenging 1,000-mile "Mille Miglia," attesting to the high standard of the vehicles and the personalities present at the event.

This year, there would be 22 classes for privately owned cars and four for commercial vehicles. The organisers did not include a motor trade class after receiving an edict from the S.M.M.T. requesting the banning of such entries. Over 260 people submitted entries, a record for this event, with 155 cars on view to the public on Devonshire Place.

Some vehicles, particularly the commercial ones, had to be positioned in Compton Street, where, with permission from the booking agency, the General Amusements Corporation Ltd., 'Bluebird' was also on display. They placed the 272-mph record-breaking car under cover, and visitors paid a small fee to view it.

All entrants received a class card and a number to attach to the front of their cars. They were required to take up their allocated positions by 10:30 a.m., with judging starting at 11:00 a.m.

This year, judges awarded marks for elegance of line (50), harmony of colours (30), and comfort and good taste (20). For commercial vehicles, marks were given for service and utility (40), general condition (30), general appearance (20), and engine cleanliness (10 marks).

A highlight of this year's show was that about two-thirds of the entries featured coachwork by renowned coachbuilders. An example was the work of Park Ward, a well-known North London firm noted for bespoke bodies that combined style with performance. Mr A. Rofe's Park Ward Rolls-Royce, which displayed bespoke automotive design and craftsmanship, won the Park Gates Hotel Challenge Bowl this year. The remaining entries showcased standard production bodywork, thus demonstrating a varied collection of styles.

Of great interest to spectators were the vehicles from the French luxury automobile and racing company, which displayed eight 30 h.p. Delage cars lined up in Devonshire Place. Each car is being driven by pretty mademoiselles from Paris.

Patrons of this year's show were the mayor of Eastbourne, Alderman Lachlan MacLachlan J.P., Lt-Col. R.V. Gwynne, D.S.O., D.L., J.P.; Captain Sir Malcolm Campbell, D.D.O., K.B.E.; Earl Howe, C.B.E., and W. Stranger-Jones.

The classes for motor vehicles attending the show:

1. Open cars costing up to £200.
2. Closed cars costing up to £200.
3. Open cars from £201 to £350
4. Closed cars from £201 to £350.
5. Open cars costing from £351 to £500.
6. Closed cars costing from £351 to £500.
7. Closed cars costing from £501 to £700.

Light Car & Cyclecar

Cpt. Eric Short, front row left. The judges at the show.

8. Closed cars costing from £701 to £1,000.

9. Closed cars priced from £1,001 to £1,250.

10. Closed cars from£1,251 to £1,500.

11. Closed cars costing over £1,500. Park Gates Hotel Challenge Trophy.

12. Open sports cars costing up to £500.

13. Closed sports cars costing up to £500.

14. Open sports cars costing over £500.

15. Closed cars costing over £500.

16. Smartest car of any value owned by a bona fide Eastbourne resident.

17. Smartest car of any value owned by a bona fide Sussex resident.

18. Most distinctive car up to the value of £500.

19. The most distinctive car costing over £500.

20. The smartest car owned & driven by a lady, costing up to £500.

21. The smartest car owned & driven by a lady costing over £500.

22. Best kept, driven and maintained by a chauffeur.

23. Smartest & best kept delivery vans up to 15 cwt.

24. Smartest and best-kept delivery vans over 15 cwt.

25. Smartest and best-kept delivery lorries.

26. Closed motor coaches.

The judges this year were with the classes they judged:

Sir Algernon Guinness, Bart. (19), Rt. Hon. Earl of March (12, 13, 14), Rt. Hon. Brian Lewis (15), Lt.-Com. Montague Graham White (19), Capt. F.W. Hartman (11), Major F.H. Bale, O.B.E., M.I.A.E. (1, 2, 3), Capt. J.S. Critchley (16, 17), Mr H.E. Symons (12, 13, 14), Capt. R. Twelvetrees (23, 24, 25, 26), Capt. T. Atkings (18), Flt-Lt. H.M. Schofield, R.A.F.O. (11), Flt-Lt. C. Clarkson (6, 7), Capt. A.D. Makins, D.F.C. (19), Capt. G.E.T. Eyston (15), Mr S.F. Edge (20, 21), Mr Reid A. Railton (4, 5), Mons. Emile Bouderie (8, 9, 10), Mr W.E. Rootes (18), Mr G.F. Heath (22), Mr R.G. Tolley, B.Sc. (23, 24, 25, 26), Mr A.G. Douglas-Clease, B.Sc. (4, 5),

Mr F.M. Charles (6, 7), Mr H.J. Butler (8, 9, 10), Mr H.W. Allingham (15), Mr H.J. Mulliner (16, 17), Mr Donald M. Healey (1, 2, 3) and Mr W.C. Bersey (20, 21).

The judges included some of the most respected designers, coachbuilders, repairers, pilots, and successful racing drivers in the automotive industry.

Although not part of the competition, the Eastbourne Fire Brigade, led by Chief Officer D.W. Spence, displayed their 1932 Merryweather motorised turntable ladder, capable of extending to 100 feet. They also displayed their 1824 water pump, the first known appliance used by Eastbourne firefighters.

The Cavendish Hotel on the Grand Parade served lunch to the judges, officials, and competitors.

Thanks to the record participation this year and good weather, the event ended with a grand parade through town at 5 p.m., followed by the Mayoress, Mrs Lachlan MacLachlan, presenting prizes.

In the evening, a grand dinner and dance were held at the Winter Garden, Devonshire Park, marking the culmination of the anniversary celebrations and reflecting Eastbourne's civic pride in these public festivities.

JUBILEE CELEBRATIONS!
GRAND CONCOURS
d'ELEGANCE BALL
Wednesday, June 14th, 1933,
AT
WINTER GARDENS,
DEVONSHIRE PARK
8.30 p.m. to 2.0 a.m.
SPECIAL ENGAGEMENT
SYDNEY WATKINSON and His BAND
(Augmented)
By kind permission of the Cavendish Hotel.
TICKETS: 3/- Single; 5/6 Double
On Sale.
BOOKING OFFICE WINTER GARDENS.

Tickets could be purchased from the Secretary, in the Judges' Room at the Cavendish Hotel, or at the Winter Garden box office at Devonshire Park.

The Rt. Hon. Lord Leconfield, the Lord Lieutenant of Sussex, joined mayors from neighbouring towns at the dinner. Sydney Watkinson and his band provided the entertainment, with festivities lasting from 8:30 p.m. to 2 a.m.

Ticket options included 10/6 for dinner and dance, or separate dance admission at 3/- for one and 5/6 for two.

At the speeches after dinner, Lt-Cmdr Grahame-White, who had been a competitor in the most important Concours d'Elegance events both in this country and abroad, remarked that no show was better organised than in Eastbourne.

On 20 June, The Motor magazine wrote, 'One of the most beautiful collections of all types and prices that has ever been assembled together in the open was to be seen in Eastbourne.'

This national praise celebrated both the event's diversity and its organisational success. The Motor also noted that Eastbourne was unique in hosting the event for four consecutive years, emphasising its ongoing dedication to automotive culture and its recognition as a premier seaside resort. They also mentioned the popularity of metal spare-wheel covers painted to match the car's bodywork.

As in previous years, local motor traders placed advertisements in the newspapers, proudly stating that they had supplied cars that had won awards at the Eastbourne show. One company involved was Waghorn's Garage of Bexhill, the Hillman agents, as reported in the Bexhill-on-Sea Observer. Another was F. Ray & Sons, a Rover dealership in Eastbourne.

See Appendix IV for a full list of the prize winners.

Concours D'Elegance

at EASTBOURNE.

OPEN 2-SEATER CLASS

1st Prize gained by S. Johnson, Esq., with a

HILLMAN MINX

(SPORTS 2-SEATER)

(Supplied by Messrs. Waghorn's Garage)

CLOSED 4-SEATER CLASS

2nd Prize gained by Mrs. L. Ainsworth, with a

HILLMAN MINX

(CLUB SALOON)

(Supplied by Messrs. Waghorn's Garage)

These Cars are on view at **Messrs. WAGHORN'S Showrooms** in **TOWN HALL SQUARE,** together with a full range of **Humber Hillman Models.**

Write or Call for a Trial Run.

S. Johnson and his Hillman Minx.

15 June Daily Mirror

Light Car & Cyclecar
Wolseley Hornet receiving their prize.

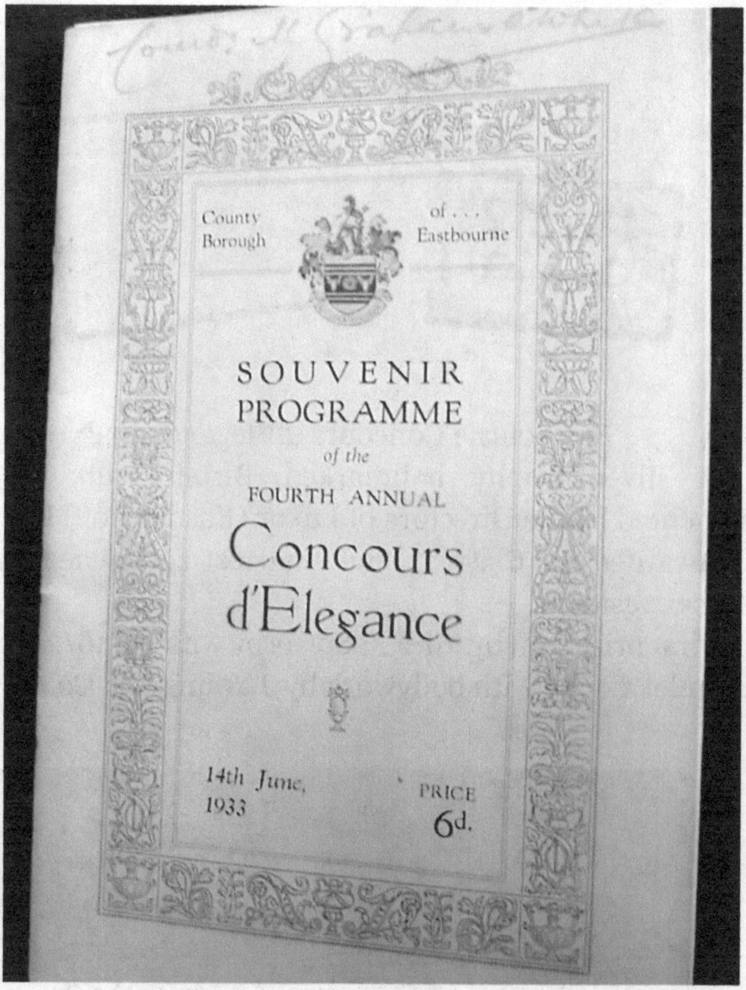

County Borough of . . . Eastbourne

SOUVENIR PROGRAMME

of the

FOURTH ANNUAL

Concours d'Elegance

14th June, 1933

PRICE 6d.

N.M.M.

Wolseley Savory

Eastbourne Concours d'Elegance 1933.

A silver trophy hallmarked Birmingham, 1930, presented by the Directors of Luxor (Eastbourne) Ltd.

Awarded for Class 17, the smartest car owned by a Sussex resident.

First prize won by Mr H.C Sowerby with his 16/20. h.p Daimler Coupe with bodywork by J Young and Co.

Light Car & Cyclecar

Winning Riley with Mrs R. Gough at the wheel. She received The Motor Cup for the most distinctive car, worth £500.

6. 27 JUNE 1934

Eastbourne's fifth annual show took place on 27 June. Last year, organisers moved the event from September to June to coincide with the Jubilee Week celebrations. Based on positive feedback from competitors, the committee decided to keep the June date, which other South Coast towns have also adopted for their own shows. This year, Mr C.J. Backshall of the Eastbourne Publicity Committee will organise and coordinate the event. The committee has decided not to include a commercial vehicle section this year. Captain E.I. Short remains chairman, and Mr E. Edgerton will serve as event secretary.

Show patrons included Eastbourne's mayor, Alderman R.G. Thornton, M.A., J.P., Lt-Col. R.V. Gwynne, D.S.O., D.L., J.P.; Captain Sir Malcolm Campbell, D.S.O.; and Sir Alan Cobham, K.B.E., A.F.C.

There were 25 classes covering all vehicle types. This year, two extra classes were added: one for ladies only, focusing on the smartest ensembles, and one for owner-driven cars priced between £300 and £750. Key judging factors included the date of manufacture and mileage. Marks awarded included 50 for body and engine cleanliness, 20 for comfort, 20 for useful fittings, and 10 for colour taste.

The entry fee was one guinea (£1 1s) per class, and only private owners were allowed to enter. Cars had to be assembled in Devonshire Place by 10:30 a.m. on the day of the show. Each participant received a class card and a number to display on their vehicle.

Judging commenced at 11:00 a.m., with 80 vehicles entered in this year's event.

The motor car classes for this year's show were:

1. Open cars costing from £150 to £250.

2. Closed cars from £150-£250.

3. Open cars from £251 to £350

4. Closed cars from £251 to £350.

5. Closed cars from £251 to £350.

6. Open cars from £251 to £350.

7. Open and closed cars from £351 to £450.

8. Closed cars from £601-£800.

9. Closed cars from £801 to £1,000.

10. No entries.

11. Closed cars from£1,251 to £1,500.

12. Closed cars costing over £1,500. (Park Gates Hotel Co. Ltd., Challenge Bowl.) 13. Open sports cars costing up to £600.

14. Closed sports car costing up to £600. (The Autocar Cup.)

15. Open sports cars over £600.

16. Closed sports cars over £600.

17. Best car owned by bona fide Eastbourne resident.

18. Best kept & smartest car of any value owned by a Sussex Resident.

19. The most distinctive car up to £600 in value.

20. The most distinctive car over £600 in value.

21. The smartest car owned and driven by a lady, up to £600 in value.

22. The smartest car owned and driven by a lady over £600 in value.

23. The smartest ensemble. Car, passengers & driver (ladies only).

24. Best kept car driven and maintained by a chauffeur (age and mileage taken into account).

25. Cars, open or closed, owner-driven, costing from £300 to £750, including extras. The Webber Trophy.

Judges for this year's show and the classes they judged: Mr George F. Heath (24, 25), Mr Donald Healey (16), Mr A.G. Douglas Clease (20), Capt. R.G. Tolley (24), Flt.-Lt. H.M. Schofield (24, 25), Capt. R. Twelvetrees (19), Hon. Brian Lewis (13, 14, 15), Mr H.J. Mulliner (8, 9, 11, 12), Capt. F.W. Hartman (19), Mr F.M. Charles (5, 6, 7), Mr H.W. Allingham (19), Lt.-Col. Warwick Wright, D.S.O., racing driver (21, 22, 23), Lt.-Col. W.C. Bersey (20), Capt. A.D. Makins, D.F.C. (5, 6, 7), Flt.-Lt. Christopher Clarkson (17, 18), Earl of March (13, 14, 15), Major F.H. Bale, O.B.E., M.I.A.E. (1, 2, 3), Capt. G.E.T. Eyston (16), Mr H.E. Symons (13, 14, 15), Mr C.J. Joyce (8, 9, 11, 12), H.E. Steiger (24, 25), managing director of General Aircraft Ltd., Croydon, Capt. T. Atkings (1, 2, 3), Miss Jose Collins, the musical comedy star(21, 22, 23), Mr W.H. Hunt (1, 2, 3), Mr H.J. Butler (24), Capt. A.W. Phillips, Mr F.S. Edge (17, 18), Lt.-Com. Grahame White, R.N. (21, 22, 23), and Earl Howe, C.B.E., P.C. (8, 9, 11, 12).

The rain likely led to fewer people attending and fewer entries being submitted this year. However, the vehicles entered were of a higher standard than in previous years. The rain stopped by 10.30 a.m., but the weather changed later in the day. Fortunately, this was after the judging and prize-giving.

Miss K. Slattery, in Class 22, the smartest car priced over £600, and owned and driven by a lady, won first prize. Her car, a 20 h.p. Alvis Speed Twenty with Vanden Plas coachwork, was eye-catching in yellow and green.

She wore a matching dress and had two red setter dogs in the car.

As usual, after the judging, the cars paraded through the town. They went along Cornfield Road, Terminus Road, Seaside Road, Cavendish Place, and along the Parade as far as the Redoubt Fort. They then headed back along the seafront to Western Lawns, where the Mayoress, Mrs Sydney Hastings, presented the prizes.

Awards for the Fifth Eastbourne Concours d'Elegance. Wednesday, June 27th, 1934.

Mrs H. Mather, Sir Malcolm Campbell's sister, won the owner-driven open or closed class and the Webber Trophy with her 12 h.p. 1914 Rover.

The car, a wedding gift, has been driven to Eastbourne and has covered more than 100,000 miles. It originally cost £350.

A car the judges liked was Captain L. F. Plugge's 20 h.p. S.S.I., painted Chinese white, with white-rimmed tyres and delicate green leather upholstery. It won three first prizes, including The Motor Trophy. S. S. Cars Ltd. was the predecessor of Jaguar Cars Limited.

Another winner, Mr Ron Yallop, a well-known racing driver from Hendon, London, driving a blue-and-cream 30 h.p. Delage Straight-8 sports saloon with bodywork by Henri Chapron of Paris, took home three firsts and trophies at Eastbourne. He then won two firsts and a second at the Bexhill event.

At the Ramsgate show, on 14 July, he received the top award, a beautiful silver rose bowl and a plaque.

The Grand Hotel held a dinner and dance in the evening, as usual. The dance started at 8:30 p.m., with tickets priced at 5/- per person. Tickets could be purchased from the secretary, Mr E. Edgerton, in the Judges' Room at the Cavendish Hotel, or at the Grand Hotel.

On 18 December 1934, an advert appeared in the Evening News in Kent for the prize-winning 1934 Lagonda 3-litre coupe-tourer, which had recently taken part in both the Eastbourne Concours d'Elegance and Ramsgate shows.

Maltby's, the coachbuilder, placed the advertisement, asking £495 for the car. They noted that the original cost had been over £800.

1934 (MARCH) Lagonda 3-litre 4-seater Coupe-Tourer by Maltby's, low mileage, a beautiful car, prize winner Eastbourne, Ramsgate Concours d'Elegance, cost over £800. £495. Maltby's, 141 Sandgate-road, Folkestone. Tel. 2261.

Another winning car from the show, entered by Mrs Cole, a blue and cream Singer 9 Le Mans that won the open vehicles up to £250 class, was available for sale. The Sussex Express published an advertisement from Alexandra Garage in Hastings on 11 December 1936, offering the car for £130.

See Appendix V for a full list of the prize winners.

1934.West Australian. Perth.W.A.

N.M.M.

The Motor

Class 21 winner. Mrs F.W. Hartman

M.Hymans

Competitors in a class for the best-dressed drivers and cars. The colour scheme was black and yellow.

Daily Mirror

7. 24 JUNE 1935

The Publicity Committee announced that they would hold the sixth annual Concours d'Elegance on Wednesday, 24 July, with no trade entries this year. As the high season for visitors, the organising committee hoped to increase tourist numbers and promote local businesses. Organisers planned two motor shows for the year: the first, the R.A.C. Rally and coachwork competition, from 26 to 30 March, followed by the Concours in late July. Despite concerns about declining interest in the Concours, the committee decided to proceed. To avoid conflicts with other motoring events, the committee chose a late July date. However, this clashed with Eastbourne's flower show, disappointing some residents. The town remained busy throughout the year, with the motor shows and the George V Silver Jubilee celebrations in May.

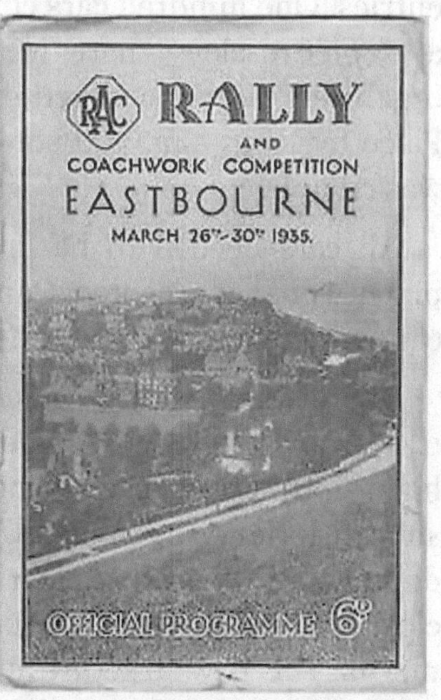

Captain E.I. Short and Mr Edgerton were the organisers; Mr B. Frank Bovill served as publicity manager. Mr Bovill also served as chief marshal.

The patrons for this year's show included the mayor of Eastbourne, Councillor Miss E.M. Thornton, J.P.; Lt.-Col. Roland V. Gwynne, D.S.O., D.L., J.P.; Captain Sir Malcolm Campbell, D.D.O.; and Sir Alan Cobham, K.B.E., A.F.C.

This year's Concours show, regarded as an important part of the motoring calendar, drew nearly 300 entries, with more cars in the larger categories and more foreign entries. One hundred cars competed, and the oldest was a 1933 Crossley. There were 22 vehicle classes, and organisers asked competitors to park in Devonshire Place by 10:15 a.m. and stay in their cars until judging was complete.

All cars needed to be properly licensed, and trade plates were not accepted. Competitors had to provide the car's catalogue price and the cost of any accessories.

There have been changes to both the competition classes and the judging system this year. The organisers have introduced eleven main classes, divided into subcategories A (open), B (two-door closed), and C (four-door closed), to ensure each body style—open, two-door closed, and four-door closed—was judged on its own merits. This new structure aims to make the competition fairer and clearer for all competitors.

The Cavendish Hotel once again served as the show's marshal and judges' headquarters, and it provided lunch.

Judging took place at 10:45 a.m. in bunting-lined Devonshire Place, as usual. This year's show adhered to the model rules established by the S.M.M.T. and R.A.C.

After the judging and the presentation of awards to successful competitors, all the vehicles, led by the prize winners, travelled through the town along the customary route: Cornfield Road, Terminus Road, Seaside Road, Cavendish Place, the Redoubt, and along the seafront to the Lawns.

Councillor Miss E.M. Thornton J.P., the mayor of Eastbourne, presented the prizes on the Lawns opposite the Grand Hotel. Again, the weather held, and it was a sunny day.

Included among the competition cups to be awarded this year were The Autocar, The Motor, and the Grand Hotel cups, as well as the Messrs William Bruford & Sons cup and the remarkably impressive Park Gates Cup. All competitors received a souvenir plaque to mark the sixth silver jubilee concours.

Mr Henry Sherek, manager of His Majesty's Theatre in London, entered his Henri Chapron-bodied Hispano-Suiza, valued at £2,250. He also arranged for Senorita Reva Reyes, the cabaret star at the "Ritz" in London and the "Casanova" in Paris, to enter the ladies' ensemble class with the car.

She did not win but accepted the Park Gates Challenge Bowl on Mr Sherek's behalf for his win in the Closed cars over £1,500 class.

The classes for motor cars attending this year's show:

2a. Open cars costing from £161-£250.

2b. Two-door closed cars costing from £161 to £250.

2c. Four-door closed cars costing from £161 to £250.

3a. Open cars costing from £251 to £350

3b. Two-door closed cars costing from £251 to £350.

3c. Four-door closed cars costing from £251 to £350.

4a. Open cars costing from £351 to £500.

4b. Two-door closed cars costing from £351 to £500.

4c. Four-door closed cars priced from £351 to £500.

5a. Open cars costing from £501 to £700.

5b. Two-door closed cars costing from £501 to £700.

5c. Four-door closed cars costing from £501 to £700.

6b. Two-door closed cars costing from $701 to £1,000.

6c. Four-door closed cars costing from £701 to £1,000.

7a. Open cars costing from £1,001 to £1,500.

7b. Closed cars priced from £1,001 to £1,500.

8. Cars costing over £1,500. Park Gates Hotel Challenge Bowl.

9b Two or four-door closed sports cars costing up to £350.

10a. Open sports car costing from £351 to £500.

10b. Two or four-door closed sports cars costing from £351 to £500.

11a. Open sports cars costing over £500.

11b. Closed sports cars costing over £500.

12. Best car owned by bona fide Eastbourne resident

13. Best kept & smartest car of any value owned by a Sussex resident.

14a. For the most distinctive open car up to £350.

14b. For the most distinctive closed car costing up to £350.

15a. For the most distinctive open car costing between £351 and £700.

15b. For the most distinctive closed car costing from £351 to £700.

16a. The most distinctive open-top car over £700.

16b. For the most distinctive closed car over £700.

17a. For a lady driver in an open or closed car costing up to £600.

17b. For a lady driver in an open or closed car costing more than £600.

18. The best ensemble. Car, passengers & driver (ladies only).

19. For chassis with two-door or four-door drophead. Occasional four-seater bodies costing up to £350.

20. For chassis with two-door or four-door drophead. Occasional four-seater bodies costing from £351 to £700.

21. For chassis with two-door or four-door drophead, occasional four-seater bodies costing over £700.

22. Best kept car driven and maintained by a chauffeur.

The judges awarded points under the headings of appearance (30), comfort (20), condition (10), general arrangement (100), interior convenience (10), ease of access (5), luggage space (5), tool layout (5), and an additional 5 marks at the judge's discretion.

N.M.M.

Judges for this year's show and the classes they judged are as follows: Hon. Brian Lewis (11a, 11b), Lt.-Com. Grahame White, R.N. (6b, 6c, 7a, 7b, 8), Lieut.-Col. Jarrott, O.B.E. (16a, 16b), Flt-Lt. Tom Rose, D.F.C. (2a, 2b, 2c), Mr George Eyston (11a, 11b), Capt. J.S. Critchley (16a, 16b), H.W. Allingham (14a, 14b, 15a), Donald Healey (2a, 2b, 2c), Flt-Lt. Christopher Clarkson (3, 3b, 3c), Mr Charles Follett (19, 20, 21), Capt. T. Atkings (15b), Flight-Lieut. C. Schofield (4a, 4b, 4c), G.F. Heath (12, 13), Capt. Rex Stocken (14a, 14b, 15a), Capt. R.G. Tolley, BSc. (3a, 3b, 3c), Capt. F.W. Hartman (17a, 17b,

18), Capt. A.W. Phillips (of the R.A.C.) (15b), Mr A.F. Palmer-Phillips (15b), H.J. Mulliner (6b, 6c, 7a, 7b, 8), F.M. Charles (5a, 5b, 5c), J.A. Masters (12, 13), W. Horsfield (9b, 10a, 10b), Alan C. Hess (4a, 4b, 4c), Mr H.E. Symons (The Times motoring correspondent) (9b, 10a, 10b), Mr A.G. Trossell (The Daily Telegraph motoring editor) (5a, 5b, 5c), and Major F.H. Bale, O.B.E., M.I.A.E. (19, 20, 21).

One of the prize winners in the Best Ladies' ensemble, for passengers and driver, was Miss P. Naismith in her gold 10/12 h.p. Standard. The car's occupants were three young ladies with dyed-gold hair. Another winner in the Sussex resident class was Miss K. Slattery, in her Alvis, which had two model retriever dogs mounted on the car's bonnet. Inside her car, she had two retrievers with matching markings.

In the evening, the Grand Hotel hosted a banquet and a dance. Tickets for both the dinner and the dance cost 12/6 and were available from the Secretary, E. Edgerton, either in the Judges' Room at the Cavendish Hotel or at the Grand Hotel.

The adagio dancers, Alexis and Dorrano, performed for the guests. As it is a Jubilee year, every competitor, whether or not they won a prize, received an inscribed plaque featuring the Eastbourne coat of arms.

Approximately 130 competitors, judges, and officials attended the dinner and dance at the Grand Hotel.

In their speeches, they thanked the Chief Constable and his police force, as well as the A.A. patrolmen who helped ensure the competition ran smoothly and without incident.

It was noted that the organising committee was nearly identical to that of 1930 and continued to secure national coverage of the Concours.

A notable entry in this year's competition was Dr John Bodkin Adams with his 1935 Armstrong-Siddeley. He did not win any prizes. Dr Adams is, of course, infamous for being accused of murdering 400 of his wealthy patients. After extensive inquiries, the police arrested him on 19 December 1956.

In January 1957, he faced trial for the murder of Edith Morrell. After 45 minutes of deliberation, the Old Bailey jury returned a verdict of not guilty.

He was later struck off the Medical Register by the GMC, but controversy over his guilt persists to this day.

See Appendix VI for a full list of the prize winners.

1931 S.S.I. Standard

M.Hymans

27 June E/B Chronicle

C. Taylor M.P.

1935 Riley 9.

8. 1 JULY 1936

The seventh annual Eastbourne Concours d'Elegance, announced in the Eastbourne Chronicle in May, was scheduled for Wednesday, 1 July. Since its first event in 1930, the Eastbourne Concours d'Elegance has successfully recreated continental European motoring competitions, showcasing the elegance and innovation of modern automotive design. Notably, Eastbourne is the only town in Great Britain to have hosted such a continuous series of events. Organisers expressed hope for the event's long future in Eastbourne. The 1936 show would open the Concours season. The organisers remained the same: Captain Eric Short as chairman, Mr Edgerton as secretary, and Mr E.F. Bovill as chief marshal. This year, the organising committee planned several important changes.

As part of this year's updates, 21 classes will be open to entrants. The prize distribution has also been revised, with awards presented by the mayor of Eastbourne, Alderman Miss E.M. Thornton, J.P., at the evening concours dinner and dance at the Grand Hotel. Ticket prices remain unchanged from last year, at 12/6d for the dinner and dance, or 5/- for the dance only.

The patrons for this year's show were the mayor of Eastbourne, Councillor Miss E.M. Thornton, J.P.; Lt.-Col. Roland V. Gwynne, D.S.O., D.L., J.P.; Captain Sir Malcolm Campbell, D.D.O.; and Sir Alan Cobham, K.B.E., A.F.C.

The classes for motor cars attending this year's show:

1a. Open cars costing up to £250.

1b. Closed cars costing up to £250.

2a. Open cars costing up to £350.

2b. Closed cars costing up to £350.

3a. Open cars costing up to £450.

3b. Closed cars costing up to £450.

4b. Closed cars costing up to £550.

5a. Closed four-door cars costing up to £750.

6c. Closed four-door cars costing up to £1,000.

7. Closed cars costing over £1,000. This class awards the Park Gates Hotel Challenge Bowl.

8a. Open sports cars priced up to £500.

8b. Closed sports cars costing up to £500.

9a. Open sports cars costing between £501 and £1,000.

10a. Open sports cars over £1,000.

10c. Closed four-door sports cars over £1,000.

11. Best car of any value owned by an Eastbourne resident. Open to both open and closed cars.

12. Best car of any value owned by a Sussex resident.

13a. Most distinctive open car costing up to £500.

13b. Most distinctive closed car costing up to £500.

14a. Most distinctive open car costing between £501 and £1,000.

14b. Most distinctive closed car costing between £501 and £1,000.

15a. Most distinctive open car over £1,000.

15b. Most distinctive closed car over £1,000. The Motor Trophy.

16a. Smartest open or closed car up to £600 owned by a lady or joint-owners.

16b. Smartest owned and driven car by a lady costing over £600.

17. Best ensemble, car, passengers & driver. This class is only open to female participants.

19. For a chassis with a 2 or 4-door drophead, 4-seater costing between £351 and £700.

20. For chassis with 2 or 4 doors, drophead, 4-seater costing over £700.

21. Best-kept car driven and maintained by a professional chauffeur.

Special Veterans class:

a. Best kept in its original condition.

b. Most attractive. Judged the most visually appealing.

Special prize for the car with the most badges.

N.M.M.

Kevin Gordon

This year, with approval from the Veteran Car Club, around 40 members and their "Old Crocks" drove down from London on 30 June.

They stopped for lunch at the Roebuck Hotel in Wychcross before continuing to Eastbourne, where they gathered at the top of Willingdon Hill before heading to Gildredge Park. Their arrival set the scene for the main show on 1 July.

On Wednesday, the organisers lined up all the vehicles in Devonshire Place, as they have in previous years, and instructed competitors to be at their designated spots by 10:15 a.m.

After the judging, which concluded around 4 p.m., the prize-winning cars received their award cards and then proceeded along Cornfield Place, Terminus Road, Seaside Road, Cavendish Place, and the seafront.

Outside the Grand Hotel, by Western Lawns, all competitors were presented with a souvenir plaque on behalf of the Eastbourne Concours d'Elegance committee.

The Hollywood Starlets, who were performing at the Dorchester Hotel in Park Lane, London, handed out these plaques. They had travelled to Eastbourne especially to attend the show.

This year, a total of 180 entries were received, with ninety-six cars competing, along with a special class for 25 vintage vehicles. There were more high-value cars on display, and the show attracted greater interest from private owners. Notably, the Parisian car manufacturer Delage brought over five vehicles specifically for the show. Organisers estimate that the value of the modern cars on display exceeded £75,000.

At this year's show, judges awarded marks for: appearance, including design and colour (30); comfort for the driver and passengers, including weather protection in open cars (20); internal condition (5); and external condition (5). General arrangement: visibility (10 marks); interior convenience, especially the position of controls (10); ease of entry and exit (5).

Additionally, for luggage-carrying capacity (5 marks); accessibility of tools (5); and special fittings, at the judges' discretion (5 marks).

Judges for the show and the classes they judged were: Lt. Comdr. Montague Grahame-White, R.N.V.R. (Veteran Car Club, President) (14b, 15a, 15b), Major F.H. Bale (14b, 15a, 15b), Major D.E.M. Douglas-Morris (13a, 13b, 14a), Capt. J.S. Critchley (16a, 16b), Capt. F.W.

Hartman (17), Capt. R.H. Stocken (14b, 15a, 15b), Capt. A.W. Phillips (11, 12), Lt-Col. W. Bersey (7); Capt. J.H. Wylie (Veteran Car Club's hon. secretary) (7), Flt-Lieut. T. Rose (1a, 1b), Mr H.J. Mulliner (13a, 13b, 14a), Mr H.E. Symons (8a, 8b, 9a, 10a, 10c), Mr D.M. Healey (1a, 1b), Mr G.F. Heath (3a, 3b), Chas Follett (4b, 5c, 6b), Mr J.A. Masters (3a, 3b), Allan C. Hess (2a, 2b), Mr G.F. Turberville (11, 12), Mr J. Nesbitt Dufont (motoring correspondent) (2a, 2b), Mr W.J. Crampton (19, 20, 21), Mr G. Bouchard (17), Mr W. Copp (19, 20, 21), Mr E.J. Girdler (8a, 8b, 9a, 10a, 10c), Mr R.H. Grant (4b, 5c, 6b), Capt. J.S. Critchley (16a, 16b), Mr K.G. Seth-Smith (16a, 16b), a pilot for the General Aircraft Co. Ltd.

Reflecting the event's spirit, many of this year's judges and competitors also participated in the inaugural Eastbourne Concours d'Elegance in 1930, highlighting the tradition and dedication of the Eastbourne Concours d'Elegance community.

As in previous years, the weather was unpredictable. It rained until midday, then cleared, only to become cloudy again in the afternoon. After judging, the competing cars toured the town as usual, driving along Cornfield Road, Terminus Road, Seaside Road, Cavendish Place, and the seafront.

Of the twelve veterans who drove from Croydon to Eastbourne, a 1902 Napier completed the 50¼-mile trip in 1 hour and 56 minutes, setting the fastest time.

Its owner, Mr G.H. Eyre, had driven it all the way from Barnsley via Penzance. After all that travelling, he won second prize in the best-kept-in-original-condition category.

1936 Daily Mirror

1936.The Telegraph, Brisbane.

He also received a silver cup for driving the longest distance to Eastbourne—430 miles—to attend the show.

The second-fastest was a 1903 12 h.p. Lanchester, which completed the journey in 1 hour and 58 minutes. Its owner, Mr F.W. Hutton-Stott, might not have been the driver of the vehicle to arrive first in Eastbourne, finishing second, but he won first prize in the veterans' best-kept and original-condition class.

See Appendix VII for a full list of the prize winners.

Medalillion presented to the veteran car entries.

The Motor

1936 2-litre M.G.

1936 Delage

THE AUTOCAR.
ADVERTISEMENTS.
JANUARY 3RD, 1936. 23
AC
Quality Cars
2 SEATER
DROP HEAD
COUPÉ
£429
DATA FOR THE DRIVER.
15.7 h.p., six cylinders, 65 × 100 m.m. (1,991 c.c.). Tax £12.
Tyres: 19 × 5 in. on knock-off wire wheels.
Timed speed over ¼ mile 83.33 m.p.h.
Acceleration from rest through the gears to 50 m.p.h., 13-2/5 sec. Acceleration from rest through the gears to 60 m.p.h., 19-2/5 sec.
Braking: 30 m.p.h. to rest in 28 feet.
Prices from £425 to £485.
A.C. (ACEDES) CARS, LTD.,
107, Park Lane, London, W.1. Works: Thames Ditton, Surrey.

9. 7 JULY 1937

The organising committee, supported by the Publicity Committee, decided that the eighth Eastbourne Concours d'Elegance would start on Wednesday, 7th July, with Captain E.I. Short as chairman. They chose July to avoid conflicting with other motoring and local events. There were 24 classes for competitors, and Mr E. Edgerton would once again act as the event's secretary.

The entry fee for competitors this year was one guinea (£1 1s). As before, a class was reserved exclusively for Eastbourne residents (Class 11). This year, the committee received 86 entries, most of which were in the higher price range. Organisers estimated that the total value of the cars displayed exceeded £91,000, an increase from last year's figure. With competitors' cars at higher values, organisers were considering introducing the Continental system in future years.

This year's patrons were the mayor of Eastbourne, Councillor J. Wheeler, J.P.; Lt.-Col. Roland V. Gwynne, D.S.O., D.L., J.P.; Captain Sir Malcolm Campbell, D.S.O.; and Sir Alan Cobham. As in previous years, the Cavendish Hotel served as the event headquarters and provided lunch for the officials.

The motor car classes for this year's show:

1a. Open cars costing up to £250.

1b. Closed cars costing up to £250.

2a. Open cars priced from £251 to £350.

2b. Closed cars costing from £251 to £350.

3a. Open cars costing from £351 to £450.

3b. Closed cars costing from £351 to £450.

4a. Open cars costing from £451 to £550.

4b. Closed cars costing from £451 to £550.

5a. Open cars costing from £551 to £750.

5b. Closed cars costing from £551 to £750.

7. Closed cars costing more than £1,000. Park Gates Hotel Challenge Bowl.

8a. Open sports cars priced up to £500.

8b. Closed sports cars costing up to £500.

9a. Open sports cars between £501 and £1,000.

10a. Open sports cars costing over £1,000.

10b. Closed sports cars costing over £1,000.

12. Smartest car owned by bona fide Sussex resident.

13a. The most distinctive open car valued up to £500.

13b. The most distinctive closed car valued up to £500.

14a. The most distinctive open car valued between £501 and £1,000.

14b. The most distinctive closed car valued between £501 and £1,000.

15a. The most distinctive open car valued over £1,000. Park Gates Hotel Challenge Bowl.

15b. The most distinctive closed car valued over £1,000. The Motor Cup.

16a. The smartest lady or joint owners' car up to £600.

16b. The smartest lady owners or joint owners' car valued at over £600.

17. The best ensemble, car, passengers & driver of any value. Ladies only.

18. The best open car of any value.

19. The best closed two-door car of any value.

20. The best four-door car of any value.

21. Void.

22. The best 2-door occasional 2-or 4-seater, any value, drop-head type.

23. The best open or closed car at any value. Continental entries only.

24. For chauffeur-driven and maintained, any value.

Captain Short again acted as chairman of the committee of twelve, with B. Francis Bovill, M.I.M.T., serving as chief marshal. The marks awarded this year were: Appearance, including design and colour (30); Comfort for both driver and passengers (20); Internal condition (5), external condition (5); general arrangement: visibility while travelling (10), interior convenience for driver and passengers (10), ease of entry and exit for driver and passengers (5), luggage carrying capacity (5), accessibility of tools (5), and, at the judge's discretion, marks for any special equipment (5).

Langney Motors displayed all the prizes at their Cornfield Road showroom on the morning of the show, allowing the public to admire them.

Chief Marshal Mr Bovill instructed all competitors to gather in Devonshire Place by 10:15 a.m. Judging commenced at 11:00 a.m. and concluded at 4:00 p.m.

N.M.M.

All competitors received a commemorative plaque for attending this year's event. As in previous years, after judging, they proceeded along Cornfield Road, Terminus Road, Seaside Road, Cavendish Place, and the seafront.

Judges for the event and the classes they judged were: Lt.-Comdr. Montague Grahame-White, R.N.V.R., (18, 19, 20), Lt.-Col. W.C. Bersey, (14b, 15a, 15b), Major F.H. Bale, O.B.E., M.I.A.E., (13b, 14a), Major D.E.M. Douglas-Morris, (3a, 3b), Capt. J.S. Critchley, (22), Capt. J.H.

Wylie, honorary secretary of the Veteran Car Club, (14b, 15a, 15b), Capt. C.G.H. Winter, (12, 13a), Flt.-Lt. Rose, D.F.C., (4a, 4b, 5a, 5b),

Sq.-Ldr. Ridley, D.S.O., (12, 13a); W.J. Crampton, (22); E.M. Wright, (10b); G.F. Heath, (23, 24); R.C. Evans, (10b); Hon. Brian Lewis, (8a, 8b, 9a, 10a); H.J. Mulliner, (18, 19, 20); Hugh P. McConnell, (13b, 14a); D.M. Healey, (8a, 8b, 9a, 10a); Chas. Follett, (4a, 4b, 5a, 5b); J.A. Masters, (7); G.F. Turberville, (7); Alan C. Hess, (16a, 16b, 17); G. Bouchard, (16a, 16b, 17); J. Douglas, (1a, 1b, 2a, 2b); E.B. Copp, (3a, 3b); E.J. Girdler, F.I.M.T., automobile engineer, (1a, 1b, 2a, 2b); and B. Page, (23, 24).

The weather was unpredictable again, with heavy rain in the morning, followed by sunny spells and a cool breeze. Many notable guests attended, including Tommy Farr, the British and Empire heavyweight boxing champion, who entered his 1937 26 h.p. Lammas Graham car with Carlton Carriage Co bodywork, which won first place in Class 5b.

Miss Mabel Constanduros, an English actress, screenwriter, and BBC Radio personality, also won first prize in Class 4b with her 1937 14 h.p. Mercedes-Benz. Mrs Doreen Phipps, née Evans, the British racing driver, was on holiday in Europe with her American racing driver husband and also entered her touring car. However, she did not win a prize.

This year, the crowds were noticeably larger, as many people hoped to see Tommy Farr and the impressive cars on display. The participation of celebrities this year and the display of high-value vehicles most likely contributed to the increase in spectators at the event.

After the introduction of a new Hillman Minx at the London Motor Show, the day before the Eastbourne Concours, Mr D. H. Noble entered the Eastbourne show and won first prize in Class 1b for closed cars under £250. Three days later, it also won two classes at the Ramsgate show.

The French company Delage was delighted with its trip across the Channel this year, as its latest cars won four first prizes in class and one second place.

Mrs Anning, driving her white 1937 40 h.p. Cord, won second prize in Class 17 for the best ensemble, passengers and driver. The upholstery of her car was navy blue, and she wore a chic sports outfit consisting of a blue skirt and a white linen coat with matching accessories.

In the evening, the Grand Hotel hosted the traditional dinner and dance, attended by about 150 guests. This year, Harry Loveday's band provided the music. Around 11 o'clock, the mayor, Councillor J. Wheeler, J.P., presented the prizes. It was a busy day for him, as he also hosted the Mayoral Garden Party in the Winter Gardens that afternoon.

During his speech at the dinner, Captain Short, the committee's chairman, proposed significant changes to the format of future events. There was disagreement over the Society of Motor Manufacturers and Traders' rules and those of the competitors. It was suggested that the current judging framework was the source of the dispute. To address this, he recommended adopting the Continental judging system, which would unify the numerous car classes into three broader categories: £500 to £1,000, £1,001 to £1,500, and over £1,500.

First, judges would assess the vehicles based on condition and design. Then, they would present the six best cars in a final review before awarding marks.

This proposal was important because it was meant to streamline the judging process, thereby reducing complexity and thus making the competition fairer and better aligned with wider European standards, reflecting shifts in both organisational practices and international influences within the field. Entry fees were the primary source of income for the Concours Committee, and this year, they amounted to £300.

Captain Short suggested that the Corporation (Eastbourne Council) should offer more financial support for the event. His remarks upset some residents, who wrote angry letters to the local newspaper expressing their frustration.

Following their success at the Eastbourne show, the Triumph Company Ltd placed a large advertisement in The Sunday Times on 11 July, announcing their first five prizes and two second places. These awards were for their 1938 models at the event. The Midland Daily Telegraph also published the advert on 14 July.

In September, Capt. Short organised an "At Home" and a Concours d'Elegance for aeroplanes at Wilmington aerodrome. At the reception, Eastbourne Corporation said, "They would spare no effort to make Wilmington the official borough aerodrome." That did not happen. The Ministry of Agriculture and Fisheries requisitioned the aerodrome during the war, and it never reopened to aircraft.

See Appendix VIII for a full list of the prize winners.

TRIUMPH

ASTOUNDING SUCCESS

with First Display of 1938 models.

5 FIRSTS AND 2 SECONDS

AT THE EASTBOURNE CONCOURS d'ELEGANCE HELD LAST THURSDAY

THE SMARTEST CARS UP TO £600. (Class 13 A. Lady Owners)
Won by 2-litre Triumph Dolomite.

THE MOST DISTINCTIVE CAR UP TO £500. (Class 13 B.)
Won by 2-litre Triumph Dolomite.
2nd - 2-litre Triumph Dolomite.

CLOSED CARS £351 to £450. (Class 3 B.)
Won by 2-litre Triumph Dolomite.

CLOSED CARS £251 to £350. (Class 2 B.)
Won by 2-litre Triumph Vitesse.
2nd - 1½-litre Triumph Dolomite.

CLOSED SPORTS CAR UP TO £500. (Class 8 B.)
Won by 2-litre Triumph Vitesse.

YOU MAY DRIVE A TRIUMPH AS HARD AS YOU LIKE FOR AS LONG AS YOU LIKE.

because all models are designed with that standard of performance in mind.

"GLORIA FOURTEEN" 6-window Saloon	£288
"VITESSE" 14/60 Sports Saloon	£298
"VITESSE" 2-litre Sports Saloon	£338
"DOLOMITE" 1½-litre Saloon	£328
"DOLOMITE" 14/60 Saloon	£348
"DOLOMITE" 2-litre Saloon	£388

1937 F.Young and his A.C. Ace class winner.

10. 1938

In October 1937, Captain Eric Short, chairman of the Concours d'Elegance committee, requested that the council double its financial support for the 1938 event from £100 to £200. He assured them that this modest increase would cover any shortfall. Captain Short emphasised the event's significant economic impact. He told them that the event consistently attracted increased funding and large numbers of visitors to Eastbourne, benefitting local businesses such as hotels, restaurants, and shops. He also said that national outlets, including newspapers, newsreels, and motoring journals, regularly featured the Concours, and that it had even been covered in Continental publications.

The Eastbourne Chamber of Commerce and Ratepayers' Association also noted that the event's extensive publicity and the business it generated far outweighed its cost to the council. Thus, they claimed the shows were enhancing Eastbourne's image and promoting economic growth. However, despite the clear economic benefits, strong community backing, and the modest financial request, The Motor magazine reported on 12 April 1938 that the Eastbourne event would not go ahead as planned. It added, "It is a pity that such a concours, which has become the leading event of its kind in the country, should be abandoned."

Capt. Short argued his case forcefully. He explained that the new show schedule would reduce the number of classes from 32 to 9, thereby lowering entry fees.

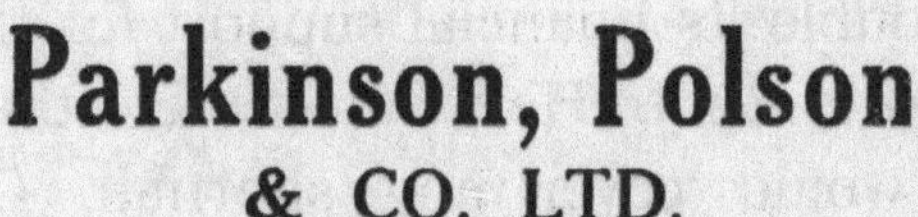

DISTRIBUTORS
for
MORRIS

MORRIS-COMMERCIAL

The

Sports

CARS

Showroom, 16 CORNFIELD ROAD
Service Depot, 30 COMMERCIAL ROAD
EASTBOURNE Phone 1924

In spite of these suggested changes, the council rejected Captain Short's proposal to increase its financial support beyond the amount already offered.

Therefore, after eight shows, all of which received high praise from motorists and the motor press, the Eastbourne Concours d'Elegance would no longer continue.

As Capt. Short noted, the cancellation meant that Eastbourne would lose not only significant national publicity and business but also the greater economic benefits and the increased profile that the event had brought to the town through tourism, media coverage, and commercial activity.

Eastbourne was fortunate to host many well-known racing drivers who had competed at Brooklands and in rallies across Ireland, France, and Italy. All of them offered their services to the Concours, serving as judges and marshals, and some also entered their own cars in the show. Sadly, the town's motor events would never again enjoy such support from such distinguished personalities.

At the Ramsgate Concours d'Elegance in July 1938, the only Concours event in England that year, Captain Short, who flew from Eastbourne to Ramsgate and served as one of the judges, stated he would never again participate in an Eastbourne event if it were conducted under the rules of the S.M.M.&T., the governing body for these competitions.

Captain Short was heavily involved with the Eastbourne Flying Club and organised a large air display in December.

His expertise helped expand Wilmington Aerodrome to accommodate 100 visiting aircraft. The council supported the aerodrome, but Short advised that it could not be designated a municipal aerodrome because it would not meet state regulations. He mentioned he had found an alternative site if the council showed interest.

In November 1938, local newspapers reported that Captain Short was to leave Eastbourne for a new role at a well-known aircraft company.

Eric Inwood Short, born in 1888 in Guildford, Surrey, served in France during WWI, where he sustained serious injuries. The army later invalided him out, deeming him unfit for active service. He moved to Eastbourne in 1922 and joined the motor dealership Caffyns, then Mansfields, and later Langney Motors.

Short was the chief supporter and organiser of the Eastbourne Concours d'Elegance on behalf of the motor car committee. He also served as chairman, organiser, honorary secretary, and a founding member of the Eastbourne Flying Club; and as a constable in the Observation Corps, Polegate.

Other roles he undertook in support of the Eastbourne community included serving as chairman of the Eastbourne Regatta for five years, as president of the Eastbourne Motor and Cycle Club, and as a sponsor of the local Air Defence Cadet Corps. Additionally, he organised the popular Concours d'Elegance for aeroplanes at the Wilmington aerodrome. Short had spent many years attempting to persuade the council to build an airport.

On news of his departure, the newspapers remarked that the town would greatly miss "his charming personality and infectious enthusiasm" and his expertise.

The Ramsgate show, held in July 1938, was the last major Concours d'Elegance event in England that year, following the cancellations of the Eastbourne and Bexhill shows. Ramsgate hosted a show in 1939, where Mr Short spoke at the Gala dinner. He expressed pride in being in Ramsgate and hoped to revive the Eastbourne Concours d'Elegance someday. The 1939 show marked the temporary end of public displays of both classic and modern cars. Notably, in the 1930s, Ramsgate was the only town in England to have hosted Concours events continuously since 1931.

As World War II approached, it would be many years before the Concours d'Elegance shows returned to Eastbourne.

During the war years (1939-1945), small airports were established across the country. After the hostilities ended, although the matter was still being discussed, the Eastbourne Council never approved plans for a commercial airport.

Captain Short died on 13 June 1946, after a brief illness at Ashford County Hospital in Middlesex.

The tradition of hosting summer motoring events in Eastbourne after the war continued, but it never matched the glamour or panache of the pre-war displays. The RAC, the BARC (July 1949), and smaller motoring clubs organised some of these events.

To bring us up to date, Eastbourne hosts the Magnificent Motors show at Western Lawns.

The "spiritual home" of motoring in Eastbourne during the May Bank Holiday weekend. Many hundreds of people attend this event, though not on the same scale as the pre-war shows.

The GARAGE FOR YOU!

Staffed and equipped to meet the varied requirements of the Motorist.

Our spacious modern Garage and Workshops have been designed to offer efficient and speedy service

CORNFIELD GARAGE LTD.
Cornfield Road
Eastbourne

Telephone 966

Managing Director: R. R. JAMES

K. Smith/The Motor

1937 Mr R. Conworth Fish and his drophead Bentley.

MAY 14, 1938 THE ILLUSTRATED LONDON NEWS 877

CECIL KIMBER ON THE RIGHT SEATING POSITION

"I want you to notice the illustration accompanying these few remarks. Driver and passengers are seated normally, yet in spite of the low build of the M.G. note how well 'in' the car they are. Only inter-axle seating and most careful designing can produce this, and you find it in all M.G. models. It keeps the centre of gravity low and obviously obviates that alarming body sway on corners that can be so frightening in a high-built car. This model, by the way, the M.G. Two-litre with the 'Tickford' all-weather body, won premier awards in each of the five Concours d'Elegance in which it was entered last year."

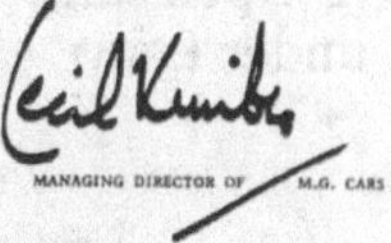

MANAGING DIRECTOR OF M.G. CARS

"BRITISH CARS ARE BETTER BUILT — BRITISH CARS LAST LONGER"

M.G. Midget Series T £222 • M.G. 1½-Litre from £280 • M.G. Two-Litre from £389 • Prices ex works. Dunlop, Triplex, Jackall

THE M.G. CAR COMPANY LIMITED · ABINGDON-ON-THAMES · BERKSHIRE · SOLE EXPORTERS — M.I.E. LIMITED · COWLEY · OXFORD · ENGLAND
4.M.

1938 advert from the M.G.Car Co.

The following pages list all the class winners, their competition numbers, the classes entered, and their car and coachbuilder details. This compilation marks the first time these details appear together.

Appendix I 1930

Private Cars Class		Entrant & Number	Year & H.P.	Car & Coach Builder
(A) Open cars under £200	1	Miss A Lorenzo (4)	1922 11.9 hp	Morris Cowley
	2	Miss K. Grimshaw (3)	1930 7 hp	Austin 7 Boyd Carpenter.
(B) Closed cars under £200	1	J.W. Hutchinson (13)	1928 15 hp	Ford Tudor Saloon
	2	W.D. Howes (15)	1930 7 hp	Triumph Super 7
(C) Open cars £200-£300	1	Mrs E. Tanner (21)	1929 20 hp	Hillman Minx
(D) Closed cars £200-£500	1	J.W. Whalley (28)	1930 12 hp	Wolseley Hornet Hoval.
	2	H. Chenevix Trench (26)	Dec 1930 18 hp	Morris Isis 15/15. Gordon England.
(E) Open cars £500-£800	1	Lord de Cliffford (36)	1930 12.9 hp	Lagonda
(F) Closed cars £500-£800	1	Miss A. Thornely (43)	1930 29 hp	Buick. Grose Ltd.
	2	F.H. Turner (40)	1930 15.7 hp	Crossley

(G) Open cars £800-£1,200	1	Mrs D. Mackle (51)	1930 20 hp	Daimler. Hoval.
(H) Closed cars £800-£1,200	1	(120) Major Willoughby-Osborne, D.S.O.	1930	Lancia (Dilambda) Farina.
	2	J. Allmann (57)	1930 25 hp	Sunbeam
(J) Closed cars £1,200 and over. The Park Gates Hotel Challenge Bowl.	1	Mrs. Churchill Wylie (58)	1929 40-50 hp	Rolls-Royce. Phantom II. Park Ward Ltd.
	2	R. Beaumont Thomas (63)	1930 40-50 hp	Rolls-Royce, Freestone & Webb.
(P.1) Smartest car owned by Eastbourne Resident.	1	Miss A. Thornely (48)	1930 29 hp	Buick. Grose Ltd.
	2	Mrs Wright-Ingle (64)	1930 20-25 hp	Rolls-Royce, Caffyns.
(P.2) Smartest car owned by Sussex resident.	1	(120) Major Willoughby-Osborne D.S.O.	1930	Lancia (Dilambda), Farina.
	2	Mrs M. White (66)	1930 40 hp	Minerva 8.
(R) Best kept owner driven.	1	Miss A. Lorenzo (4)	Oct 1922 11.9 hp	Morris Cowley
	2	Mrs Boord (50)	July 1927 30 hp	Packard

Commercial Vehicles				
(L) Smartest Delivery Vans & best kept.	1	Southern Publishing Co, Ltd. (86)	1930 24 hp	Ford Light Van
	2	Frowd's Dairies Ltd. (76)	1926 11.9 hp	Morris
(M) Smartest Lorries & best kept.	1	Messrs Mansfields Ltd. (113)	1929 17.9 hp	Dennis
	2	Messrs Pickfords Ltd. (114)	1927 36 hp	Leyland
(N) Smartest & best kept Open motor coaches.	1	Southern Glideway Coaches Ltd. (115)	1930	Leyland Tiger, Duple.
	2	Southdown Motor Services Ltd. (116)	1930	Tilling-Stevens, Harringtons.
(O) Smartest & best kept Closed motor coaches.	1	Southdown Motor Services Ltd. (118)	1930	Leyland Tiger, Harringtons.
	2	Southern Glideway Coaches Ltd. (117)	1930	Gilford, Duple.

Appendix II 1931

Private Cars Class		Entrant & Number	Year & H.P.	Car & Coach Builder
(A&B) Open & closed cars up to £150		Void		
(C) Closed cars £151 - £250	1	H.H. Anspach (1)	1931 7 h.p.	Austin. Swallow.
	2	R.H. Parson (5)	1931 9 h.p.	A.J.S. A.J.Stevens.
(D) Open cars £151- £250	1	H.R. Malling (14)	1931 12 h.p.	Wolseley Hornet. Swallow.
	2	R.H. Rice (15)	1931 12 h.p.	Wolseley Hornet Swallow.
	3	H.L. Wardle (8)	1931 8 h.p.	M.G. Jarvis & Sons
(E) Closed cars £251 £350	1	W. Gilling (32)	1931 9 h.p.	Riley
	2	Lillian Butchart (23)	1931 9 h.p.	Riley
(F) Open cars £251- £350	1	A.P. Dundas (34)	1931 16 h.p.	Austin
(G) Open & closed cars £351 - £450	1	Dr P.W. Mathew (41)	1931 16 h.p.	Humber

	2	H. Chenevix Trench (37)	1929 16 h.p.	Morris Isis. Gordon England.
(H) Open & closed cars £451 - £800	1	Lady Malcolm Campbell (45)	1931 18 h.p.	Talbot 75
	2	C. Brocklehurst (48)	1931 18 h.p.	Talbot
	3	Mrs E.A. Cummings (46)	1931 19.3 h.p.	Rover
(I) Open & closed cars £801 - £1,000	1	E.O. Hobden (66)	1931 20 h.p.	Armstrong Siddeley. Young & Co.
	2	Arthur F. Davis (72)	1931 18 h.p.	Talbot 90 Martin Walter,
(J) Open & closed cars £1,001 - £1,700	1	Lincoln Motor Co (86)	1931 40 h.p.	Lincoln
	2	Arthur Wheeler (78)	1928 25 h.p.	Bentley. Vanden Plas.
	3	David H Murray (84)	1931 29.4 h.p.	Delage. Chapron.
(K) Open & closed cars costing over £1,700. Park Gates Hotel Challenge Bowl.	1	Lady Malcolm Campbell (94)	1931 44 h.p.	Rolls-Royce. H.J. Mulliner.
	2	Mrs Churchill-Wylie (92)	1931 44 h.p.	Rolls-Royce Park Ward.

(L) Open & closed sports cars under £500	1	P. Lucas (100)	1931 8 h.p.	M.G Midget
	2	Mrs A.P. Watson (26)	1931 16 h.p.	Standard. Avon.
(M) Open & closed sports cars over £500	1	G.F. Earle (85)	1931 28 h.p.	Bentley. Harrison & Sons.
	2	Leon Bachelier (103)	1929 17.8 h.p.	Bugatti
(N) Smartest car Eastbourne Resident.	1	Lady Foley (91)	1930 44 h.p.	Rolls-Royce. Barker.
	2	Mrs A.P. Watson (26)	1931 16 h.p.	Standard. Avon.
(O) Smartest car Sussex resident.	1	J. Carter (109)	1931 25 h. p	Rolls-Royce 20-25 Thrupp & Mabberley.
	2	Harold Heal (93)	1931 25 h.p.	Rolls-Royce Mulliner.
(P)Most distinctive car. The Motor cup.	1	R.G. Edwards (90)	1931 45 h.p.	Isotta-Fraschini Cesare Sala.
	2	R. Beaumont-Thomas (99)	1931 45 h.p.	Bentley. Freestone & Webb.
(Q) Best kept owner-driven.	1	Mrs W. Mather (111)	1914 13.9 h.p. 80,000 miles.	Rover.

	2	Mrs Churchill-Wylie (47)	1923 18 h.p. 94,538 miles.	Armstrong Siddeley Burlington.
(R) Best chauffeur-driven car.	1	C. Brocklehurst (49)	1927 16 h.p. 40,000 miles.	Wolseley. Hamshaws.
	2	Arthur Wheeler (78)	1928 25 h.p. 27,208 miles.	Bentley. Vanden Plas.
(S) Veteran cars before 1904.	1	Captain de S. Colver (125)	1896 3½ h.p.	Carl Benz. 1st car used in Ireland.
	2	Sydney G. Cummings (116)	1900 5 h.p.	Peugeot 190 Freres.
(T) Open & closed cars up to £500. Previous 1st award winners in a Concours.	1	Miss Paddie Naismith (157)	1931 9 h.p.	Standard Nine. Avon.
(U) Open & closed cars £501-£1,000 Previous 1st award winners in a Concours.	1	Lt.-Col. Willoughby Osborne, D.S.O. (161)	1930 32 h.p.	Lancia-Delambde Farina.
(V) Open & closed cars costing over £1,000.		Previous 1st award winners in a Concourse.	Cancelled	

(W) Most distinctive car, any value in classes T,U,V.	1	Mrs Raymond Gough (159)	1930 17.9 h.p.	M.G. Brainsbury.
	2	Lt.-Col. Willoughby Osborne, D.S.O. (161)	1930 32 h.p.	Lancia-Delambde Farina.
<u>Trade Vehicles</u>				
(X) Smartest & best kept delivery vans.	1	Southern Publishing Co. (167)	1930 24.9 h.p.	Ford
	2	A. Downs & Sons (176)	1930 6.3 h.p.	Chevrolet Spurlings.
(Y) Smartest & best kept Lorries.	1	Lex Garages Ltd (185)	1931 26.3 h.p.	Bedford Spurlings.
	2	Trinidad Leaseholds Ltd (188)	1931 38 h.p.	Leyland. Tinker.
(Z) Smartest & best kept closed motor coaches	1	Southdown Motor Services Ltd (194)	1930	Leyland Tiger. Harrington's

1929-1932 M-Type M.G. Midget.

Appendix III 1932

Private Cars Class.		Entrant & Number	Year & H.P.	Car & Coach Builder
(1) Closed car £150 to £250	1	A.H. Oxenford (5)	1933 12 h.p.	Standard 12
	2	Mrs O.E. Wybrants (1)	1932 9 h.p.	Standard 9
(2) Open cars £150 to £250.	1	H.L. Wardle (11)	1931 8 h.p.	M.G. Midget, Jarvis.
	2	W.J.B. Richardson (8)	1932 9 h.p.	Singer Nine
(3) Closed cars £251 to £350	1	Miss L. Roper (16)	1932 12 h.p.	Armstong Siddeley Charlesworth.
	2	C.G. Quinton (17)	1932 12 h.p.	M.G. Magna 12, Abbey.
(4) Open cars £251 to £350.	1	F.H. Redfern (20)	1932 9 h.p.	Wolseley Hornet, Maltby
(5) Open & closed cars £351 to £500	1	Major A.D. Carey (32)	1931 14 h.p.	Riley Alpine 6
	2	C.D. Siddeley (25)	1932 15 h.p.	Armstrong Siddeley
(6) Open & Closed cars £501 to £700	1	H.P. Henry (48)	1932 20 h.p.	Armstrong Siddeley

	2	W.M. Couper (42)	1932 12.8.h. p	Lagonda
(7) Open & Closed cars £701 to £1,000	1	Mrs H.S. Eaton (59)	1932 21 h.p.	Alpine Talbot 105 Vanden Plas.
	2	Noel Rees (62)	1932 21 h.p.	Talbot 105. Wylders..
(8) Open & Closed cars £1,001 to £1,500	1	Lady Malcolm Campbell (65)	1932 25 h.p.	Rolls-Royce Gurney Nutting.
	2	Miss B. Spell (73)	1932 30 h.p.	Delage. Letourneur.
(9) Open & Closed cars over £1,500. Park Gates Hotel Challenge Bowl.	1	A. Webber (75)	1932 50 h.p.	Daimler 40-50 Martin Walter.
(10) Open & closed Sports cars up to £350	1	C.G. Quinton (17)	1932 12 h.p.	M.G. Magna. Abbey.
(11) Open & closed Sports cars over £350	1	Mrs H. Eaton (59)	1932 21 h.p.	Talbot 105. Vanden Plas.
	2	A. Gruzelier (66)	1932 29 h.p.	Delage. Figoni.

(12) Smartest car any value owned by an Eastbourne resident	1	R.C. Fish (81)	1932 20 h.p.	Sunbeam. Freestone & Webb.
	2	Mrs R. Selby (76)	1927 45 h.p.	Isotta Fraschini. Cesare Sala.
(13) Smartest car any value owned by Sussex resident	1	Major M. Cohn (78)	1932 13.9 h.p.	Lagonda
	2	Mrs K. Pearce (46)	1933 16 h.p.	Sunbeam
(14) Most distinctive car of any value. The Motor Trophy.	1	J.R. Scott (33)	1932 14 h.p.	Talbot 65. Darracq.
	2	A. Webber (75)	1932 30 h.p.	Daimler. Martin Walker.
	3	Mrs B Selby (76)	1927 45 h.p.	Isotta Fraschini.
(15) Smartest car owned and driven by a lady	1	Mrs H. Eaton (59)	1932 21 h.p.	Talbot 105. Vanden Plas.
	2	Miss B. Spell (73)	1932 30 h.p.	Delage. Letourneur.
	3	Mrs Hamilton-Fleming (70)	1931 25 h.p.	Daimler. Mulliner.

(16) Best-kept chauffeur-driven	1	Miss R.A. Garside (86)	1932 12.8 h.p.	Rover Pilot
	2	R.H. Hill (45)	1932 15-18 h.p.	Lanchester. Mulliner (Birmingham).
(17) Smartest Riley owner-driven and maintained		Cancelled		
(18) Smartest Wolseley Hornet owner-driven and maintained	1	Miss C. Labouchere (89)	1932 12 h.p.	Wolseley Hornet Daytona. Eustace Watkins.
	2	Major D.E.M. Douglas Morris (14)	1931 12 h.p.	Wolseley Hornet coupé. Salmons.
<u>Trade Classes</u>				
(19) Closed cars £150 to £250	1	Mansfields Ltd (91)	1933 10 h.p.	Hillman Minx, Salmons.
(20) Open cars £150 to £250		(21) Closed cars £251-£350	both	Cancelled
(22) Open cars £251 to £350	1	Fox & Nicholls Ltd (95)	1932 12 h.p.	Wolseley Hornet, Abbey Coachworks.

(23) Open & closed cars £351-£500	1	Lendrum & Hartman Ltd (99)	1932 35 h.p.	Buick. General Motors Ltd.
(24) Open & closed cars £501-£700	1	Dunkley & Davidson Ltd (104)	1932 20 h.p.	Armstong Siddeley
(25) Open & closed cars costing £701 to £1,000	1	Rootes Ltd (109)	1932 24 h.p.	Humber Pullman Thrupp & Maberly.
(26) Open & closed cars costing £1,001-£1,500	1	Ford Motor Co (112)	1932 51 h.p.	Lincoln. H.J. Mulliner.
(27) Open & closed cars		over £1,500		Cancelled
(28) Open & closed Sports cars up to £350	1	Kevill-Davies & March Ltd (115)	1932 12 h.p.	Wolseley Hornet March Special, Whittingham.
	2	M.G Car Co Ltd (114)	1933 8 h.p.	J-Type M.G. Midget, Carbodies.
(29) Open & closed Sports cars over £351		Cancelled		
(30) Most distinctive car up to £500	1	Arrow Coachworks Ltd (96)	1932 12 h.p.	Wolseley Hornet, Arrow
(31) Most distinctive car over £500	1	Rootes Ltd (109)	1932 24 h.p.	Humber Pullman. Thrupp & Maberly.

(32) Most distinctive car with specialised coachwork	1	Rootes Ltd (109)	1932 24 h.p.	Humber Pullman. Thrupp & Maberly.
(33) Delivery vans, smartest and best kept.	1	Southern Publishing Co Ltd. (122)	1930 24 h.p.	Ford
	2	G.K. Maynard Ltd (116)	1932 26 h.p.	Bedford. Spurlings
(34) Lorries, smartest and best kept	1	Trinidad Leaseholds Ltd (132)	1932 45 h.p.	Leyland. Steel Barrel.
	2	Eastbourne Gas Co. (129)	1920 20 h.p.	Vulcan. Lockwood's.
(35) Motor coaches (closed) smartest & best Kept.	1	Farnham Blue Coaches Ltd. (135)	1932 36 h.p.	Gilford. Abbott.

1932 Daimler Double Six

Appendix IV 1933

Private Cars Class		Entrant & Number	Year & H.P.	Car & Coach Builder
(1) Open cars up to £200.	1	S. Johnson (2)	1933 10 h. p	Hillman Minx Carbodies Sports, 2-seater.
	2	R.E. Hotchkiss (4)	1933 10 h. p	Hillman Minx
(2) Closed cars up to £200	1	Mrs C. Spikins (14)	1933 9 h. p	Singer 9 Sports Coupe.
	2	Mrs L. Ainsworth (13)	1933 10 h. p	Hilman Minx Club saloon.
(3) Open cars £201-£350	1	J.A. Steel (21)	1933 20 h.p.	S.S.I. Swallow.
		Mrs N. Olive (25)	1933 20 h.p.	S.S.1. Swallow.
	2	Miss H. Astbury (20)	1933 12 h.p.	M.G. Magna
(4) Closed cars £201-£350	1	Mrs E. Tanner (29)	1933 16 h.p.	S.S.I. Swallow.
	2	R.M. Ponder (38)	1933 16 h.p.	S.S.I. Swallow.
(5) Open cars £351-£500	1	R. Merton (49)	1933 15 h.p.	Daimler. Strachan's.
(6) Closed cars £351-£500	1	Miss I.C. Shwedler (61)	1933 14 h.p.	Rover Speed Pilot
	2	W.W. Smyth (57)	1933 15 h.p.	Daimler. Stratstone.

(7) Open cars £501-£700	1	Mrs K.S. Skinner (70)	1933 24 hp	Humber Snipe
	2	Major K.S. Savory (67)	21-60 h.p.	Wolseley. Carlton Carriage.
(8) Closed cars between £701-£1,000	1	Miss A.M. Sykes (84)	1933 20 hp	Alvis Speed 20. Thrupp & Maberly.
	2	A.W.G. Parfremen (79)	1933 21 h.p.	Talbot. Vanden Plas.
(9) Closed cars £1,001-£1,250	1	Mrs H. Clayton (87)	1933 21 h.p.	Lagonda
(10) Closed cars £1,251-£1,500	1	Miss E.M. Nickson (95)	1932 30 hp	Delage. Lancefield.
	2	Mrs W.H. Kingsmill (94)	1932 30 h.p.	Delage. Henri Chapron
(11) Closed cars over £1.500 Park Gates Hotel Challenge Bowl.	1	A. Rofe (103)	1933 20-25 h.p.	Rolls-Royce. Park Ward.
	2	F. Bilton (100)	1932 50 h.p.	Rolls-Royce. Park Ward.
(12) Open sports cars up to £500	1	J.A. Steel (21)	1933 20 h.p.	S.S.I. Swallow.
	2	F. Van Praugh (109)	1933 12 h.p.	Wolseley Hornet. Patrick Motors.
(13) Closed sports cars up to £500	1	E. Ainsworth (37)	1933 20 h.p.	Standard Avon New Avon.

	2	F.H. Winter (112)	1933 12 h.p.	Alvis Firefly
(14) Open sports cars over £500	1	J.A. Steel (116)	1933 20 h.p.	Alvis Speed 20. Charlesworth.
	2	Major M. Cohn (118)	1933 16-80 h.p.	Lagonda. Vanden Plas.
(15) Closed sports cars over £500	1	S. Gootnick (90)	1932 30 h.p.	Delage. J. Figoni.
	2	A.V.G. Parfrement (79)	1933 21 h.p.	Talbot. Vanden Plas.
(16) Smartest car owned by Eastbourne resident	1	G. Tansley (125)	1927 25 h.p.	Daimler. Maythorn & Sons.
	2	R.C. Fish (122)	1932 20 h.p.	Sunbeam. Freestone & Webb.
(17) Smartest car owned by Sussex resident.	1	H.C. Sowerby (81)	1932 20 h.p.	Daimler. J.Young & Co.
	2	Major M. Cohn (118)	1933 16-80 h.p.	Lagona. Vanden Plas.
(18) Most distinctive car costing up to £500 The Motor cup.	1	Mrs R. Gough (43)	1933 9 h.p.	Riley Nine
	2	E. Ainsworth (37)	1933 20 h.p.	Standard Avon. New Avon body.

(19) Most distinctive car costing over £500	1	Miss E.M. Nickson (95)	1932 30 h.p.	Delage. Lancefield.
	2	Lady M. Campbell (194)	1933 40-50 h.p.	Rolls-Royce. Barker & Co.
(20) Smartest car costing up to £500 owned and driven by a lady.	1	Miss I.C. Schwedler (61)	1933 14 h.p.	Rover "Hastings" Coupé
	2	Mrs F. Garstin (44)	1933 10 h.p.	Rover 10 Coupé. Salmonds.
(21) Smartest car costing over £500 owned and driven by a lady.	1	Miss E.M. Nickson (95)	1932 30 h.p.	Straight Delage. Lancefield.
	2	Mrs C. Gordon	16/80 h.p.	Lagonda
(22) Best kept car driven and maintained by a chauffeur.	1	F. Wilson-Hutton- Stott (130)	1924 23 h.p.	Lanchester
	2	Sir G. Beaumont (97)	1933 30 h.p.	Delage. Fernandez.

Commercial Vehicles				
(23) Smartest Delivery vans & best kept, up to 15 cwt.	1	Plummer Roddis Ltd. (139)	1933 13 h.p.	Austin. Barton & Tipper.
	2	Margery Daw. (136)	1933 14 h. p	Morris
(24) Smartest Delivery vans & best kept, over 15 cwt.	1	Hovis Ltd. (147)	1932 90 h.p.	Leyland. Hovis.
	2	Eastbourne Electricity Dept. (144)	1932 27 h.p.	Bedford. Mansfields
(25) Delivery lorries, smartest & best kept.	1	Eastbourne Electricity Dept. (154)	1932 27 h.p.	Bedford. Parrott & Higgins.
(26) Smartest & best kept closed motor coaches.	1	Southdown Motor Services Ltd.	1933 30 h.p.	Leyland Tiger. Harrington's.

1933 Wolseley Hornet

Appendix V 1934

Private Cars Class		Entrant & Number	Year & H.P.	Car & Coach Builder
(1) Open cars 150-£250.	1	Mrs P.L. Cole (4)	1933 9 h.p.	Singer 9 Le Mans
(2) Closed cars costing £150-£250. The Parkinson Cup.	1	R.F. Arnatt (6)	1934 9 h.p.	Singer.9 Coupé
	2	F.H. Jefferis (5)	1934 9 h.p.	Singer.9 Coupé
(3) Open cars costing £251-£350	1	R. Morton-Ponder (15)	1934 16 h.p.	S.S.I. Swallow.
(4) Closed cars £251-£350. The Philco Cup.	1	Capt. L.F. Plugge (25)	1934 20 h.p.	S.S.I. Standard. Swallow.
	2	Miss A. Thornely (29)	1934 12 h.p.	Humber Vogue.
	3	Major A.D. Carey (28)	1934 20 h.p.	S.S.I. Swallow.
(5) Open cars costing £351-£450	1	Col. A.H. Loughborough R.A. (37)	1934 14 h.p.	Rover Speed.14
(6) Closed cars £351-£450. The Grand Hotel Cup.	1	Mrs E. Langlands	12 h.p.	M.G. Magnette. Abbey.

	2	Miss I.C. Schwedler (42)	1933 14 h.p.	Rover.
(7) Closed cars £451-£600	1	R.M. Cardwell	12 h.p.	M.G. Magnette. Abbey.
	2	Mrs. F.W. Hartman (53)	1934 28 h.p.	Buick. Gen Motors of Canada.
(8) Closed cars £601-£800	1	C.E. Shingles (54)	1933 20 h.p.	Alvis. Charlesworth.
(9) Closed cars £801-£1,000	1	Major M.D. Cohn (57)	1934 30 h.p.	Lagonda Coupé. Lancefield.
(10) Closed cars £1,001-£1,250		No entries.		
(11) Closed cars costing £1,251-£1,500	1	R.A. Yallop (61)	1934 30 h.p.	Delage D8 Coupé H. Chapron.
(12) Closed cars over £1.500. Park Gates Hotel Challenge bowl.	1	A. Webber (68)	1932 50 h.p.	Double-Six Daimler. Gurney Nutting.
	2	A.H. Beadle (64)	1934 30 h.p.	Delage. Figoni.
(13) Open sports car costing up to £600	1	Col. A.H. Loughborough, R.A. (37)	1934 14 h.p.	Rover

(14) Closed sports cars costing up to £600. The Autocar Cup.	1	Capt. L.F. Plugge (25)	1934 20 h.p.	S.S. I. Swallow.
	2	Major A.D. Carey (28)	1934 20 h.p.	S.S.I. Swallow.
(15) Open sports cars cover £600	1	R.C. Fish (73)	1934 30 h.p.	Lagonda. Freestone & Webb.
	2	Major M.D. Cohn (57)	30 h.p.	Lagonda. Lancefield.
(16) Closed sports cars over £600	1	R.A. Yallop (61)	1934 30.h.p.	Delage D8 Coupé. H.Chapron.
	2	S.E. Sears	26 h.p.	Bentley. Salmons & Sons.
(17) Smartest car owned by an Eastbourne Resident.	1	R.C. Fish (73)	1934 30 h.p.	Lagonda. Freestone & Webb.
(18) Smartest car owned by a Sussex resident. The Mayne Cup.	1	Major.M.D. Cohn (57)	1934 30 h.p.	Lagonda Coupé. Lancefield.
	2	Mrs F.H. Hartman (53)	1934 28.2 h.p.	Buick. Gen Motors of Canada.

(19) Most distinctive car up to £600 in value. The Motor Trophy.	1	Capt.L.F. Plugge (25)	1934 20 h.p.	S.S.I. Swallow.
	2	Miss.A.Thornely (29)	1934 12 h.p.	Humber Vogue
(20) Most distinctive car over £600 in value. The Mayor's Cup.	1	R.A. Yallop (61)	1934 30 h.p.	Delage D8 Coupé. H. Chapron.
	2	A. Gibbs (77)	1934 25 h.p.	Bentley. Barker & Co..
(21) Smartest car up to £600 owned and driven by a lady. The Bruford Cup.	1	Mrs F.W. Hartman (53)	1934 28.2 h.p.	Buick. Gen Motors of Canada.
	2	Mrs Nancie Olive (27)	1934 10 h.p.	Standard. Avon.
(22) Smartest car over £600 owned and driven by a lady.	1	Miss K. Slattery (60)	1934 20 h.p.	Alvis Speed. Vanden Plas.

(23) Smartest Ensemble-car, passengers & driver (ladies only).	1	Mrs D. Masters (74)	1934 21 h.p.	Talbot. E.D. Abbott.
	2	Mrs Nancie Olive (27)	1934 10. h.p.	Standard. Avon.
(24) Best kept car driven and maintained by a chauffeur.	1	F.H. Winter (71)	1933 12 h.p.	Alvis
(25) Open or closed cars costing £300-£750, owner-driven & extras. The Webber Trophy.	1	Mrs H. Mather (47)	1914 12 h.p.	Rover 12
	2	Miss L.M. Roper (34)	1932 12 h.p.	Armstrong - Siddeley. Charlesworth.

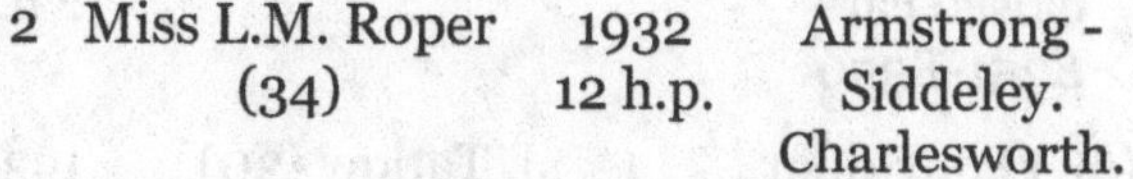

Delage D8 Coupé. H. Chapron body.

Appendix VI 1935

Private Cars Class		Entrant & Number	Year & H.P.	Car & Coach Builder
(2A) Open cars between £161-£250	1	J.K. Maynard (3)	1935 10 h. p	Hillman Minx Sports 2-seater. Cross & Ellis.
(2B) Two-door closed cars £161-£250	1	Mrs K. Petre (6)	1935 12 h.p.	Morris Series II Coupé
	2	Miss.I.M. Burton (4)	1935 14 h.p.	Vauxhall
(2C) Four-door closed cars £161-£250	1	H. Parkinson (11)	1935 10 h.p.	Morris
(3a) Open cars £251-£350	1	Miss J. Astbury (14)	1935 20 h.p.	S.S.I.
(3b) Two-door closed cars £251-£350	1	D.H. Noble (15)	1935 12 h.p.	Humber
(3C) Four-door closed cars £251-£350. The Parkinson Cup.	1	J. Tatlow (30)	1935 12 h.p.	Riley
	2	Mrs E.M. Wisdom (23)	1935 21 h.p.	Morris
(4a) Open cars £351-£500	1	H. Wolfe (34)	1935 22 h.p.	Terraplane. Hudson Motors.

(4b) Two-door closed cars £351-£500	1	R.T. Smith (36)	1935 20 h.p.	S.S.I.
(4c) Four-door closed cars £351-£500..	1	H. Cooper (46) The Grand Hotel Cup	1935 14 h.p.	Rover
	2	J.E.G. Powell (41)	1935 25 h.p.	Studebaker
(5a) Open cars £501-£700	1	L. Prideaux-Brune (56)	1935 12 h.p.	Aston-Martin. Bertelli.
(5b) Two-door closed cars £501-£700	1	J.F.H. Harper (59)	1935 29 h.p.	Railton. Coachcraft.
(5c) Four-door closed cars £501-£700	1	W.M. Couper (64)	1935 18 h.p.	Talbot. Darracq.
(6b) Two-door £701-£1,000	1	W.C. Wells (67)	1935 20 hp	Alvis. Vanden Plas.
(6c) Four-door closed cars £701-£1,000	1	K. Carr (72)	1935 28 h.p.	Hotchkiss. Lancefield.
(7a) Open cars between £1,001-£1,500	1	A.F. Lawson (74)	1934 30 h.p.	Delage. Letourneur & Marchand.
(7b) Closed cars £1,001-£1,500. The Motor cup.	1	Mrs. H.W. Graesser-Thomas (75)	1935 37 h.p.	Stutz. Bransby Woolard.
(8) Closed cars over £1.500. Park Gates Hotel Challenge Bowl	1	H. Sherek (96)	1935 37 h.p.	Hispano-Suiza. Chapron.

	2	C.W. Evans (79)	1934 25 h.p.	Rolls-Royce. Windovers.
(9b) 2 & 4 doors closed sport cars up to £350	1	F.D. Cooper (27)	1935 14 h.p.	Rover
(10a) Open sports cars £351-£500	1	S.G. Marshall (32)	1935 12 h.p.	Riley
(10b) 2 & 4 door closed sports cars £351-£500	1	H. Cooper (46)	1925 14 h.p.	Rover
	2	R.A. Morris (39)	1934 16 h.p.	S.S.I.
(11a) Open sports cars over £500	1	R. Conworth Fish (83)	1935 25 h.p.	Bentley. H.J. Mulliner.
	2	Mrs K.H. Wilson (84)	1935 28 h.p.	Delage. Fernandez.
(11b) Closed sport cars over £500	1	W.F. Watson (87)	1935 25 h.p.	Bentley. Freestone & Webb.
	2	H. Sherek (96)	1935 37 h.p.	Hispano-Suiza. Chapron.
(12) Smartest car owned by an Eastbourne resident. The Courier Cup.	1	C.W. Evans (79)	1934 25 h.p.	Rolls-Royce. Windovers.
(13) Smartest car owned by a Sussex resident. The Bruford Cup.	1	L.C. Cohen (91)	1934 20 h.p.	Alvis. Vanden Plas.

Class	Place	Entrant	Year / h.p.	Make
	2	Miss K. Slattery (68)	1934 20 h.p.	Alvis. VandenPlas.
(14a) Most distinctive open car costing up to £350	1	Miss J. Astbury (14)	1935 20 h.p.	S.S.I.
(14B) Most distinctive closed car costing up to £350	1	R.F. Arnett (29)	1935 10 h.p.	Triumph
	2	Mrs L.F. Dyer (12)	1935 10 h.p.	Morris
(15a) Most distinctive open car £351-£700	1	P. Ellison (82)	1935 16 h.p.	A.C.
(15b) Most distinctive closed car £351-£700	1	Miss M. Gilling (48)	1935 12 h.p.	Riley
	2	R.T. Smith (36)	1935 20 h.p.	S.S.I.
(16a) Most distinctive open class over £700	1	R. Conway Fish (83)	1935 25 h.p.	Bentley. H.J. Mulliner.

(16b) Most distinctive closed car over £700. The Motor trophy.	1	J.L.F. Stedman (80)	1935 25 h.p.	Rolls-Royce. Young & Co.
	2	W.F. Watson (87)	1935 25 h.p.	Bentley. Freestone & Webb.
<u>Lady driver only</u>				
(17a) Open or closed car up to £600	1	Miss S.J. Longheed Baskin (92)	1934 20 h.p.	S.S.I.
	2	Mrs M. Grose (54)	1934 20 h.p.	Vauxhall. Grose.
(17b) Open or closed car over £600. The Vigrod Trophy.	1	Mrs D. Masters (89)	1935 30 h.p.	Auburn
(18) Best ensemble, driver & passengers.	1	Mrs K.H. Wilson (84)	1935 \28 h.p.	Delage. Fernandez.
	2	Miss P. Naismith (8)	1935 10-12 h.p.	Standard
(19) For chassis: 2- or 4-door drophead, up to £350; occasional 4-seater bodies.	1	J.K. Maynard (3)	1935 10 h.p.	Hillman Minx. Cross & Ellis.
(20) From £351-£700. The Autocar Trophy.	1	J.F.K. Harper ((59)	1935 29 h.p.	Railton. Coachcraft.

	2	L. Prideaux-Brune (56)	1935 12 h.p.	Aston Martin. Bertelli.
(21) Over £700	1	R. Conway Fish (83)	1935 25 h.p.	Bentley. H.J. Mulliner.
(22) Chauffeur-driven and maintained. The Arthur Webber Trophy.	1	C.W. Evans (79)	1934 25 h.p.	Rolls--Royce. Windovers.
	2	F.S. Winter (63)	1935 24 h.p.	Humber

1935 Studz

Appendix VII 1936

Private Cars. Class		Entrant & Number	Year & H.P.	Car & Coach Builder
(1a) Open cars costing up to £250	1	Lt.-Comdr. A.J.S. Eastley (2)	1936 12 h.p.	Standard Avon. New Avon Body Co Ltd.
(1b) Closed cars costing up to £250	1	Miss.A. Talibart (8)	1936 12 h.p.	Standard
(2a) Open cars costing Up to £350	1	Mrs N. Haylock (13)	1936 10 h.p.	Triumph
(2b) Closed cars costing up to £350.	1	F.D. Cooper (16)	1935 14 h.p.	Rover
	2	J.D. Ouvry (20)	1935 14 h.p.	Rover
(3a) Open cars costing up to £450	1	Col. A.H. Loughborough R.A. (31)	1934 14 h.p.	Rover
(3b) Closed cars costing up to £450	1	Miss D. Evans (49)	1936 18 h.p.	M.G.
	2	Mrs T. Rose (45)	1936 16 h.p.	Triumph
(4b) Closed cars costing up to £550	1	C.E. Harrington (40)	1936 20 h.p.	S.S. Jaguar
(5a) Closed four-door cars up to £750	1	Mrs D. Masters (55)	1935 30 h.p.	Auburn

(6b) Closed four-door cars up to £1,000	1	C.G. Dunham (57)	1936 24 h.p.	Talbot. Clement.
(7) Closed cars costing over £1,000. Park Gates Hotel Challenge Bowl.	1	G.F. French (68)	1936 25 h.p.	Rolls-Royce. Freestone & Webb.
	2	Col. R. Rippon (62)	1936 27 h.p.	Humber. Ribbon Bros.
(8a) Open sports car costing up to £500	1	Col. A.H. Loughborough, R.A. (31)	1934 14 h.p.	Rover
(8b) Closed sports cars costing up to £500	1	C.H. Cooper (41)	1935 14 h.p.	Rover
(9a) Open sports cars between £501-£1,000	1	Miss M.D. Patten (78)	1936 20 h.p.	British Salmson
(10a) Open sports cars over £1,000	1	R. Conworth Fish (80)	1934 25 h.p.	Bentley. H.J.Mulliner.
(10c) Closed four-door sports cars over £1,000	1	E. Streather (82)	1936 25 h.p.	Bentley. Park Ward.
(11) Best car, any value owned by an Eastbourne resident.	1	R. Conworth Fish (80)	1934 25 h.p.	Bentley. H.J. Mulliner.

(12) Best car, any value owned by a Sussex resident.	1	E. Streather (82)	1936 25 h.p.	Bentley. Park Ward.
(13a) Most distinctive open car up to value £500	1	J.E. Scott (14)	1936 10 h.p.	Talbot. Whittingham & Mitchell.
(13b) Most distinctive closed car up value £500	1	C.E. Harrington (40)	1936 20 h.p.	S.S. Jaguar
	2	Miss L.M. Roper (23)	1936 10 h.p.	Triumph. Cross & Ellis.
(14a) Most distinctive open car £501-£1,000	1	Major G. Bradstock D.S.O. M.C. (56)	1936 28 h.p.	Railton. Coachcraft.
(14b) Most distinctive closed car £501-£1,000	1	La Baronne de Fontanges (92)	1936 24 h.p.	Delage. Letourneur & Marchand.
(15a) Most distinctive open car over £1,000	1	R. Conworth-Fish (80)	1934 25 h.p.	Bentley. H.J. Mulliner.
(15b) Most distinctive closed car over £1,000. The Motor Trophy.	1	Mde. P. Cartier (95)	1936 31 h.p.	Delage. De Villars.
	1	Miss K. Slattery (60)	1936 25 h.p.	Alvis. Gurney Nutting.
	2	H. Owen (74)	1936 25 h.p.	Bentley. H.R. Owen.

(16a) Smartest car costing up to £600 owned and driven by a lady.	1	Mrs T. Rose (45)	1936 16 h.p.	Triumph
	2	Miss L.M. Roper (23)	1936 10 h.p.	Triumph. Cross & Ellis.
(16b) Smartest car costing over £600 owned and driven by a lady.	1	Mde. Richer-Delavau (94)	1936 26 h.p.	Delage. Figoni.
	2	Mrs D. Constant (66)	1935 25 h.p.	Rolls-Royce. H.J.Mulliner.
(17) Best ensemble-car, driver & passengers (ladies only).	1	Mde. P. Cartier (95)	1936 30 h.p.	Delage. De Villars.
	2	La Baronne de Fontanges (92)	1936 24 h.p.	Delage. Letourneur & Marchand.
(19) Best 2-or 4-door, 4-seater, drophead costing £351-£700	1	J.R. Maudslay (52)	1936 20 h.p.	Standard Avon. New Avon Body Co.
(20) Best 2- or 4-door, 4-seater, drophead costing over £700	1	R. Conway-Fish (80)	1934 25 h.p.	Bentley. H.J.Mulliner.

(21) Best kept car driven and maintained by a chauffeur.	1	C.W. Evans (65)	1935 25 h.p.	Rolls-Royce. Windovers.
(a)Best kept, in original condition.	1	F.W. Hutton-Stott Jnr. (115)	1903 12 h.p.	Lanchester
	2	G.N. Eyre (110)	1902 19.6 h.p.	Napier
(b) Most attractive.	1	Major G.W.G. Allen (103)	1899 6 h.p.	Daimler
	2	Capt. J.H. Wylie (113)	1903 6 h.p.	Wolseley
Special prize for the car with most badges.		H.C. Dryden (12)	1935 9 h.p.	Riley

1936 Delage D6 60

Appendix VIII 1937

Private Cars Class		Entrant & Number	Year & H.P.	Car & Coach Builder
(1a) Open cars costing up to £250	1	E.J. Owers (2)	1937 10 h. p	Talbot 10. Clement.
(1B) Closed cars costing up to £250	1	D.H. Noble (8)	1937 10 h.p.	Hillman Minx
(2a) Open cars £251-£350	1	W.P. Maidens (11)	1937 12 h.p.	Rover 12
(2B) Closed cars costing between £251-£350	1	F.W. Billingham (19)	1937 2 litres 16 h.p.	Triumph Vitesse
	2	A.S. Osborne (21)	1937 1 ½ litre 14 h.p.	Triumph Dolomite
(3a) Open cars between £351-£450	1	Mrs A. Girdler (24)	1937 2 litres. 18 h.p.	M.G. Salmons & Sons.
(3B) Closed cars between £351-£450	1	M. Newnham (28)	1938 2 litres 16 h.p.	Triumph Dolomite
	2	C.H. Cooper (27)	1937 20 h.p.	Rover
(4a) Open cars £451-£550	1	H.F. Young (36)	1937 16 h.p.	A.C. Ace

(4b) Closed cars £451-£550	1	Miss Mabel Constanduros	1937 14 h.p.	Mercedes-Benz
(5a) Open cars £551-£750	1	Major G. Bradstock (43)	1937 24 h.p.	Delage D6 70. Coachcraft.
(5b) Closed cars between £551-£750	1	T. Farr (49)	1937 26 h.p.	Lammas Graham. Carlton Carr Co
(7) Closed cars over £1,000.	1	Jack Barclay (57)	1937 51 h.p.	Rolls-Royce Phantom III. Park Ward.
	2	Mrs A.P. Good (66)	1937 30 h.p.	Lagonda
(8a) Open sports cars up to £500	1	W.P. Maidens (11)	1937 12 h.p.	Rover
(8B) Closed sports cars up to £500	1	F.W. Billingham (19)	1937 2 litres 16 h.p.	Triumph Vitesse
(9a) Open sports cars £501-£1,000	1	Mrs E. Fane (41)	1937 16 h.p.	Frazer-Nash. B.M.W.
(10a) Open sports cars over £1,000	1	Viscount Curzon (74)	1937 30 h.p.	Lagonda Rapide
(10b) Closed sports cars over £1,000.	1	Hugh C. Hunter (76)	1936 4½ litre 30 h.p.	Derby Bentley Sports Coupé. Vanden Plas.
	2	Jack Barclay (57)	1937 51 h.p.	Rolls-Royce Phantom III. Park-Ward.

(11) Smartest car owned by Eastbourne Resident.	1	Void		
(12) Smartest car owned by a Sussex resident.	1	R. Conworth Fish (71)	1937 25 h.p.	Bentley. HJ. Mulliner.
	2	Dr St. John Lyburn (85)	1937 20 h.p.	S.S. Jaguar
(13a) Most distinctive open car costing up to £500	1	H.F. Young (36)	1937 16 h.p.	A.C. Ace
(13B) Most distinctive closed car costing up to £500	1	Mrs E. Rose (31)	1937 2 litres 16 h.p.	Triumph Dolomite
	2	M. Newnham (28)	1937 2 litres 16 h.p.	Triumph Dolomite
(14a) Most distinctive open car £500-£1,000	1	Miss V. Levinge (52)	1937 24 h.p.	Delage D6 70. Marcel Pourtout.
(14b) Most distinctive closed car £500-£1,000	1	Mrs E.G. Daniels (50)	1937 30 h.p.	Hudson. Coachcraft.

(15a) Most distinctive open car over £1,000. The Park Gates Hotel challenge Bowl.	1	R. Conworth Fish (71)	1937 25 h.p.	Bentley. H.J.Mulliner.
(15b) Most distinctive closed car over £1,000. The Motor Trophy.	1	Hugh C. Hunter (76)	1936 4½ litre 30 h.p.	Bentley. Vanden-Plas.
	2	Mde Richer-Delavau (60)	1937 32 h.p.	Delage D8 100. Franay.
<u>Lady driver only</u>				
(16A) Open or closed car up to £600	1	Mrs E. Rose (31)	1937 2 litres 16 h.p.	Triumph Dolomite
(16b) Open or closed car over £600	1	Mrs A.P. Good (66)	1937 30 h.p.	Lagonda
(17) Best ensemble, passengers & driver.	1	Miss K. Slattery (83)	1936 25 h.p.	Alvis. Gurney Nutting.
	2	Mrs D. Anning (72)	1937 40 h.p.	Cord

(18) Best open car of any value.	1	Mde de Laborderie-Rollet (79)	1937 32 h.p.	Delage D8 120. De Villars
	2	R. Conworth Fish (71)	1937 25 h.p.	Bentley. H.J.Mulliner.
(19) Best closed two-door car.	1	Hugh C. Hunter (76)	1936 4½ litre 30 h.p.	Derby Bentley. Vanden-Plas.
(20) Best closed four-door car.	1	J. Barclay (57)	1937 51 h.p.	Rolls-Royce Phantom III. Park-Ward.
	2	Col. R. Rippon (56)	1937 29 h.p.	Railton. Rippon Bros.
(22) Best two-door, 2/4-seater, drop head.	1	R. Conworth Fish (71)	1937 25 h.p.	Bentley. H.J.Mulliner.
	2	L. Appleton (63)	1935 30 h.p.	Bentley. James Young & Co.
(23) Continental entries only; Best open or closed car of any value.	1	Mde de Laborderie-Rollet (79)	1937 32 h.p.	Delage D8 100. de Villars.
(24) Chauffeur-driven and maintained.	1	Mrs F.A. Wright-Ingle (78)	1935 25 h.p.	Rolls-Royce. Hooper.

Autocar

1937 Mrs Rose's Triumph Dolomite

1937 Mr Young's A.C.

1937 Jack Barclay's 2 first and second cups.

Stirling silver trophies. - main one hallmarked H.J. Lias & Sons, London 1878, 26 cm high, weighing 487 grams.

The smaller ones are marked 'Birmingham, 1936' and 'Birmingham, 1937'.

ABOUT THE AUTHOR

Stephen LeVine was born in London and educated in Hove and London. After many years of travelling around the world, working for a holiday tour company, he returned to England. He established his own business in 1985, moved to Hailsham, Sussex, and became a resident of Eastbourne in 1987. With a keen interest in history, he has also written articles for the local history society.

Other titles by the author:

Lords to Bureaucrats:
A History of Sussex Town Halls and their local benefactors.

Hailsham Barracks: 1803 – 1815

Unsung Heroes:
Eastbourne's Fire Service 1824-1974

The Sitakund Disaster:
A story of fire and explosions in the English Channel in 1968.

Pacific Mystery:
A tale of rumour, missing gold and pirates.

Six ships, one name:
All named Eastbourne, including Royal Navy vessels.

For King or Country:
Major Philip Van Cortlandt, 1739-1814: A memoir.

Tides of Courage:

The remarkable life of Harry Diplock.

www.ingramcontent.com/pod-product-compliance
Lightning Source LLC
LaVergne TN
LVHW030912080826
845145LV00010B/2866
* 9 7 8 0 9 9 3 5 4 4 1 8 7 *